Brush Up
Your Poetry!

Brush Up Your Poetry!

Michael Macrone

ILLUSTRATIONS BY TOM LULEVITCH

CADER BOOKS
NEW YORK

Andrews and McMeel
A Universal Press Syndicate Company
Kansas City

THANK YOU for buying this Cader Book—we hope you enjoy it. And thanks as well to the store that sold you this, and the hardworking sales rep who sold it to them. It takes a lot of people to make a book. Here are some of the many who were instrumental:

Editorial:
Rufus Griscom, Jake Morrissey, Dorothy O'Brien, Regan Brown

Design:
Charles Kreloff, Orit Mardkha-Tenzer

Copy Editing/Proofing:
Linda Olle, Jack Murnighan

Production:
Carol Coe, Cathy Kirkland

Legal:
Renee Schwartz, Esq.

Copyright © 1996
Michael Macrone and Cader Company Inc.
All rights reserved. No part of this book may be used or reproduced in any manner whatsoever without written permission of the Publisher. Printed in the United States of America.

If you would like to share any thoughts about this book,
or are interested in other books by us, please write to:

CADER BOOKS
38 E. 29 Street
New York, NY 10016
Or visit our cool new web site: http://**www.caderbooks.com**

Library of Congress Cataloging-in-Publication Data
Macrone, Michael.
Brush up your poetry! / by Michael Macrone. — 1st ed.
p.   cm.
Includes index.
ISBN 0-8362-2145-1
1. English poetry. 2. American poetry. 3. English poetry—Explication. 4. American poetry—Explication.   I. Title
PR1175.M22   1996
821.008—dc20   96-43989

November 1996
First edition
10 9 8 7 6 5 4 3 2 1

ATTENTION: SCHOOLS AND BUSINESSES
Andrews and McMeel books are available at quantity discounts with bulk purchase for educational, business, or sales promotional use. For information, please write to: Special Sales Department, Andrews and McMeel, 4520 Main Street, Kansas City, Missouri 64111.

Contents

Introduction

Poetry is as old as Western culture itself. Our earliest narratives—including the Hebrew Bible and the works of Homer—are written in verse. For centuries, poetry was synonymous with literature; practically every great literary work, and most minor ones, were verse: the Greek drama, the Classical epics, *The Divine Comedy,* Shakespeare's plays and sonnets—all are written in verse.

Poetry obviously doesn't get the respect it used to. There's been a recent revival of interest, in cafés, in bookstores, and even on television. But for many, poetry is just something they were forced to read in school. They find it difficult and pretentious, or vague and melodramatic. Poetry still has prestige, but few read or speak it.

At least, few *realize* they're speaking it. Hardly a day goes by when you don't either hear or quote a poetic phrase. It might not even sound like verse—take "getting and spending," coined by William Wordsworth, or "in one ear and out the other," by Chaucer. You may associate poetry with metaphors and symbols, such as Eliot's wasteland or Poe's croaking raven. But more often cited are the everyday truths well said, elegant yet direct: "truth is stranger than fiction" (Lord Byron), "fools rush in where angels fear to tread" (Alexander Pope), or "things fall apart" (W. B. Yeats).

It should be no surprise poetry has lent the English language hundreds of quotable phrases. Poets, after all, are experts in saying things well. And while it's been quite some time since you could call it "popular," poetry was once more widely read and absorbed, more often quoted from memory, and thus more tightly woven into spoken English.

We take for granted such sayings as "bolt upright," "play with fire," and "ignorance is bliss." But once they were fresh and exciting, sharp and unworn. My aim in *Brush Up Your Poetry!* is to bring some of these sayings back home and back to life. Everyday phrases and quotable lines are traced to the source and presented in context. I cite short passages and explain how they work, and I try to recapture the spirit of their time and place.

Along the way, I also touch on literary history and suggest how to read poems, but this isn't English class. I try to keep the proceedings lively, because poetry is the liveliest literature. To experience that—to experience the energy and excitement of poetry—is to understand most of its meaning.

The phrases and poems are grouped by poet. A select group of prolific and influential figures (Shakespeare, for example) get chapters to themselves. The rest are gathered into chronological chapters. I begin with Geoffrey Chaucer, the great ancestor of English verse, and stop just short of World War II with the Modernist poets. Much has been left out, of course, including good lines and great poets; this is a brush, not a sweep. I hope it inspires you to seek for more.

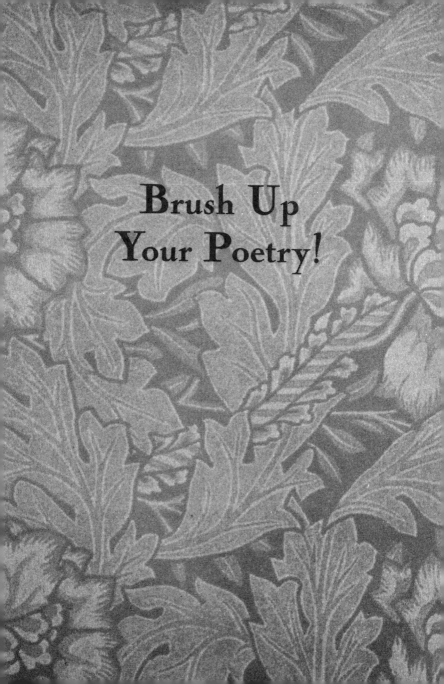

Brush Up Your Poetry!

Geoffrey Chaucer

Geoffrey Chaucer (ca. 1343–1400), one of English poetry's biggest guns, isn't the classroom staple he used to be. This is partly his fault for writing in Middle English; kids today have a hard enough time with their own language. And where Chaucer is taught, students usually read one of those uninspiring modern "translations," which make Chaucer's verse seem quaint, if not silly. Modern spelling alone—with its implied pronunciation—can turn what's beautiful and strange in the original into something laughable. Fortunately, Chaucer's poetry is so compelling and so entertaining that many readers continue, with the help of notes and glossaries, to enjoy him in the original. The more they read, the easier—and in fact more pleasurable—the language becomes.

At the top of the canon, of course, are the unfinished *Canterbury Tales,* which Chaucer began in the 1380s and continued to work on to his death. Like Boccaccio's *Decameron,* a slightly earlier and similar work, Chaucer's *Tales* are stories within a story. The premise is a holy pilgrimage by thirty people from London to Canterbury, where St. Thomas à Becket was martyred. These fictitious pilgrims tell the tales themselves, each more or less appropriate to the teller (and some of them slightly obscene). Chaucer planned to write four stories for each pilgrim, but only twenty-four tales survive, two of them partial.

What's amazing about the *Tales* is not that they're all terrific (indeed, some are tedious); it's that they're so diverse in subject, style, and thought. The material is rarely original; Chaucer was happy to borrow (or outright steal) from other poets and storytellers. Chaucer was great not by virtue of originality, but because he embodied in verse the fullness of his time—the voices and the attitudes, the excitement and the boredom, the nobility and the baseness, the sacred and the profane. And, like the more original Dante, he did so in the people's tongue, rather than in the elite's.

In 1400 French was the language of the English court, and so it would remain until Prince Hal became Henry V. Though raised the son of a vintner, Chaucer spent most of his life serving one or another of the royal tribe, including King Edward III. As page to a prince, valet to a king, and trade emissary to Italy, Chaucer learned plenty of languages while adapting to the customs and thinking of a wide range of characters. In this regard he was much like Shakespeare, another commoner become servant to the Crown, and another poet of incomparable stylistic and human range.

We know much less of Chaucer's literary life than we know of his official life. Dates of composition are uncertain, and of course there are no printed records—Gutenberg was only three years old when Chaucer died. Besides an armful of manuscripts of varying quality, we have only a few portraits, including one engraving of Chaucer reciting at a lectern, presumably to a courtly crowd. We can't see what manuscript he's reading from; it would likely have been from a more conventional work than the *Tales.*

Few people beyond English majors are familiar with Chaucer's lesser works, some of them "lesser" only by comparison with the best *Canterbury* poems. Chief among these is *Troilus and Criseyde,* an adaptation from Boccaccio's *Il Filostrato* and one source for Shakespeare's *Troilus and Cressida.* Chaucer's version is by far the most stylish, which is to say most Italian, poem written in Middle English. Other minor works are also worthwhile, especially *The House of Fame, The Book of the Duchess,* and *The Parliament of Fowls,* though one is liable to grow more impatient with the language because their content isn't nearly so appealing to modern taste.

In the following survey of Chaucerian coinages I present the original passages in Chaucer's English, with an accompanying rough modern translation. (I make no effort to preserve the poetry, only to strike a balance between literalness and comprehensibility.) Quotations and citations follow the text of F. N. Robinson's *Works of Geoffrey Chaucer,* 2nd edition (Houghton Mifflin, 1957). Passages from *The Canterbury Tales* are identified by fragment (lettered A through G) and line number. (The order of these fragments differs in various manuscripts.)

A note on pronunciation

To hear the music of Chaucer's verse, you need to know how his English was spoken. Since there are no cassette recordings from the period, we mostly have to guess the sounds, based on spelling and the position of Middle English relative to its Germanic and French ancestors.

Most differences from modern English pronunciation lie in the vowels. Consonants have held pretty steady, though Chaucer's contemporaries pronounced some that have since become silent—the k and g of *knyght,* for example. Vowels are a little trickier, and the differences between one *a* and another subtle. Here's a rough guide:

a is generally pronounced like the *a* in *father,* and never like the *a* in *make.*

e, when long, is similar to the *a* in *make*; when short, it's like the *e* in *bed.* The *e* at the end of a word such as *soote* ("sweet") is pronounced lightly.

i, when long, is similar to the *i* in *pique*; when short, it's like the *i* in *tip.*

o, when long, is like our long *o* but sometimes like the *o* in *trough*; when short, it's like the *o* in *top.* When followed by *u, w,* or *gh,* it sounds like the *u* in *truth.*

u by itself is similar to the *u* in *put.*

y is the same as *i.*

Double vowels like *aa* and *ee* are pronounced as the long form of the single vowel.

Middle English diphthongs—vowel combinations such as *au* and *ou*—are less slurred than ours. In general, they sound like the long form of the first vowel plus the short form of the second.

The famous illustration of how to pronounce Chaucer's English is line 43 of the *General Prologue* to the *Canterbury Tales*: "A Knyght ther was, and that a worthy man." You can pronounce it more or less this way:

Ah k-neekt thahr wahss, ahnd thaht a worthee mahnn.

To get some real idea of what this sounds like, you may wish to check out one of the many readings available on record or tape. (CDs will be harder to find.)

Whan That Aprill with His Shoures Soote...

Whan that Aprill with his shoures soote
The droghte of March hath perced to the roote,
And bathed every veyne in swich licour
Of which vertu engendred is the flour;
Whan Zephirus eek with his sweete breeth
Inspired hath in every holt and heeth
The tendre croppes, and the yonge sonne
Hath in the Ram his halve cours yronne,
And smale foweles maken melodye,
That slepen al the nyght with open ye
(So priketh hem nature in hir corages);
Thanne longen folk to goon on pilgrimages,
And palmeres for to seken straunge strondes,
To ferne halwes, kowthe in sondry londes;
And specially from every shires ende
Of Engelond to Caunterbury they wende,
The hooly blisful martir for to seke,
That hem hath holpen whan that they were
    seke.

The Canterbury Tales:
General Prologue, A.1–18

When April with its showers sweet
The drought of March has pierced to the root,
And bathed every vein in such moisture
By whose power engendered is the flower;
When Zephyrus also with his sweet breath
Has inspired in every holt and heath
The tender crops, and the young sun
Has run half his course in the Ram,
And small birds make melody,

That sleep all the night with open eye
(So Nature pricks them in their hearts);
Then folk long to go on pilgrimages,
And palmers to seek strange strands,
To distant hallows, known in sundry lands;
And specially from every shire's end
Of England to Canterbury they wend,
The holy blissful martyr for to seek,
That has helped them when they were sick.

At 128 words—a 7-bit sentence—this is the most famous long-winded introduction in English poetry. (The adverbial "when" clause, at 79 words, sets a record all by itself.)

But the stanza is also fluid and musical, like the sweet *licour* of spring that flows over the land. Chaucer begins his poem in the season of beginnings, mid-April, when showers bathe awakening Nature, when *Zephyrus* (the West Wind) breathes life into crops, when the sun is completing its arc through Aries, when the nightingales are alive with desire in the night. It is at this time of awakening, the poet says, that "longen folk to goon on pilgrimages."

By *longen* Chaucer means "desire." In some cases this longing was born of holy devotion, inspiring pilgrims to make the long trek, on foot and on horseback, to the Canterbury shrine of St. Thomas à Becket. Thomas, a victim of King Henry II's power struggle with the Church establishment, had become a national symbol for devotion to faith. His shrine in time took on a sort of magical healing quality, which also attracted some of the pilgrims (*palmers*). Others, as Chaucer's portraits reveal, went along out of more earthly motives.

◈

A Knyght Ther Was...

A Knyght ther was, and that a worthy man,
That fro the tyme that he first bigan
To riden out, he loved chivalrie,
Trouthe and honour, fredom and curteisie.

The Canterbury Tales:
General Prologue, A.43–46

A knight there was, a worthy man,
That, from the time he first began
To ride out, loved chivalry,
Truth and honor, freedom and courtesy.

After setting the scene of the Canterbury pilgrimage, Chaucer introduces the pilgrims, deferentially beginning at the top of the social ladder. The nameless Knight, highest in rank, is also the most accomplished member of the merry band. He's both an avid warrior and a sophisticated gentleman, equally schooled in chivalry and "courtesy," which in Chaucer's usage means "courtly demeanor."

The Knight is also privileged to tell the first tale, which turns out to be just the sort of story a chivalrous knight would tell at court. Most of the tales are likewise suited to their tellers, though Chaucer didn't necessarily write them to order. A few stories appear to have lain in a dusty pile before Chaucer "repurposed" them.

Freshly composed or not (the Knight's probably was), each tale serves a dual purpose. First, it entertains or edifies unto itself; second, it figures in the larger story of the pilgrimage. Some characters use their stories to attack one another, or to justify themselves, or to illustrate an attitude. That is, each tale reflects somehow on its teller.

Thus to really appreciate the stories, you have to know something about the characters, whom Chaucer introduces in the *General Prologue*. Here are the characters we'll meet, in order of their appearance in the prologue:

The Narrator—Chaucer himself, or rather a semi-fictitious Chaucer; not only is the pilgrimage a fiction, Chaucer the narrator is more naive than Chaucer the author, which is the principal source of the *Prologue's* irony.

The Knight—A perfect gentleman and a fighting Christian.

The Prioress [*Nonne*]— Madame Eglantine, a somewhat affected woman, whose religious devotion is less evident than her devotion to etiquette (*curteisie*) and her pet dogs. Madame also wears a gold brooch inscribed with the pagan motto *Amor vincit omnia* ("Love conquers all," coined by Ovid). She isn't the last of Chaucer's clerical characters more interested in material pleasures than they ought to be.

The Monk—A man with advanced ideas on the subject of monkhood. For example, he doesn't care much either for study or for work, and he mocks silly old-fashioned restrictions. Mostly, he likes rabbit hunting.

The Merchant—The token bourgeois, full of pomposity and practical advice though not financially stable himself.

The Clerk—Not a bank teller but a philosophy student at Oxford; impoverished and dour, he cares for nothing but learning. Chaucer's contemporaries actually considered this virtuous.

The Franklin—Chaucer's *franklin* (landholding commoner) is a wealthy devotee of luxury, "Epicurous owene sone" (A.336).

The Wife of Bath—Chaucer's best-loved character, the spicy wife has a powerful sense of her own rights and pleasures. She's had five husbands (since age 12) and is very pleased to report that she ultimately mastered at least four of them.

The Miller—An oxlike figure of a man, given to running his head through doors. Second only to the Wife of Bath in readers' hearts, despite (or perhaps because of) the fact that he's a profane braggart and cheat.

The Reeve—A feudal bureaucrat, originally a carpenter, thin and choleric, but a careful and savvy overseer of his lord's manor, not to mention a successful speculator on his own behalf.

The Host—Harry Bailey, proprietor of the Tabard, an inn in London's Southwark district. A merry and sporting man, he inspires the *Tales* by proposing a story-telling contest to while away the journey to Canterbury.

The Canon—The Canon (member of a religious fraternity specially bound to the canons of the Church) is one of the shadier characters in the *Tales*. A learned alchemist—which is to say snake-oil salesman—he may be on the run from a victim when he encounters the pilgrims.

The Canon's Yeoman—The Canon's loose-lipped right-hand man. Once he starts to blab, the Canon stealthily makes off.

The other 20 characters are the Squire, the Yeoman, the Second Nun, the Nun's Priest, the Monk, the Friar, the Man of Law, the Haberdasher, the Carpenter, the Weaver, the Dyer, the Tapestry-Maker, the Cook, the Shipman, the Doctor of Medicine, the Parson, the Plowman, the Manciple, the Summoner, and the Pardoner.

As Lean as a Rake

A Clerk ther was of Oxenford also,
That unto logyk hadde longe ygo.
As leene was his hors as is a rake,
And he nas nat right fat, I undertake,
But looked holwe, and therto sobrely.

The Canterbury Tales:
General Prologue, A.285–89

There was also a clerk of Oxford,
who had long been studying logic.
His horse was as lean as a rake,
And neither was he very fat, I'd say,
But looked hollow, and grave about it.

The Clerk is Chaucer's starving student, a scholar of logic, which at the time was a major branch of learning, though fairly useless unless you had a theological career in mind. Actually, all university students were pledged to become *clerics,* of which *clerks* is an abbreviation; that our clerk has been at his logic for so long may indicate lack of enthusiasm for the bargain.

No matter; his austere poverty expresses a love for learning and a disdain for worldly pursuits, or what we would call today "a real job." So far from fat that he's concave, the Clerk is obviously not eating well, nor happy about it: there are limits to his worldly disdain.

Though his is the earliest citation in the *OED,* Chaucer may not have coined this phrase—it sounds very much like a folk saying. But the origins of phrases are rarely certain, and there's no strong literary argument that he couldn't have coined it. So let's just say he did.

Every Man for Himself

"We stryve as dide the houndes for the boon;
They foughte al day, and yet hir part was noon.
Ther cam a kyte, whil that they were so wrothe,
And baar awey the boon bitwixte hem bothe.
And therfore, at the kynges court, my brother,
Ech man for hymself, ther is noon other.
Love, if thee list, for I love and ay shall;
And soothly, leeve brother, this is al."

The Canterbury Tales:
The Knight's Tale, A.1177–84

"We strive as did the dogs for the bone;
They fought all day, and yet won nothing.
There came a kite, while they were warring,
And bore away the bone from between them.
And therefore, as at the king's court, my brother,
Each man for himself, there is nothing else.
Love, if you wish, for I love and always shall;
And truly, dear brother, this is all."

Chaucer's knight "loved chivalrie," which is the subject of his tale. The plot involves a rivalry between two noble kinsmen; the theme is courtly love.

Cousins Palamon and Arcite of Thebes, having fought on the losing side of a battle with Athens, are taken prisoner. After being locked in a tower for a few years with no prospect of release, they're about as low as noble youths can be. But it only gets worse when, one fine day in May, they spy a radiant maiden in the garden.

As it turns out, this maiden, Emily, is the sister-in-law of Athens's king Theseus (who becomes a "duke" in the knight's telling). Though set so far beyond their romantic means, Emily inspires in each the same desire, and the same lack of chivalrous deference. As Arcite puts it, the operative attitude is "Ech man for hymself, ther is noon other."

Their ensuing struggle over the "rights" to Emily has its moments of pathos, inspiring many great verses. But it also has a ridiculous side; the supposed "nobility" of the

cousins, along with the whole idea of "nobility" in general, are put to tests they don't entirely pass, as Chaucer (if not the knight) is well aware.

To Knit One's Brow

This Palamon, whan he tho wordes herde,
Despitously he looked and answerde,
"Wheither seistow this in ernest or in pley?"
    "Nay," quod Arcite, "in ernest, by my fey!
God helpe me so, me list ful yvele pleye."
    This Palamon gan knytte his browes tweye.
"It nere," quod he, "to thee no greet honour
For to be fals, ne for to be traitour
To me, that am thy cosyn and thy brother...."

The Canterbury Tales:
The Knight's Tale, A.1123–31

Palamon, when he heard those words,
Looked angrily and answered,
"Do you say this in earnest or in play?"
    "Nay," said Arcite, "in earnest, by my faith!
So help me God, I hate to play."
    Palamon began to knit his two brows.
"It were," said he, "no great honor for you
To be false, nor to be a traitor
To me, that am thy cousin and thy brother...."

As London's former controller of customs and subsidy of wools, skins, and hides, Chaucer knew a thing or two about knitting. So why does he coin the phrase as "knit his two brows" (could there be more?), when we say simply "knit his brow"?

Actually, it's the modern version that doesn't make much sense. "Knit his brow" sounds like "knit his sweater," when what we mean is "knit his two eyebrows together," which is more or less what Chaucer says. What happened is that *brow* came to mean "the ridge over one's eyes," that is, both eyebrows plus the space (if any) in between. (It was first used in this sense around 1535.) So what we mean by "knit one's brow" is to "angle together the two halves of one's brow," a considerably more complicated metaphor than Chaucer's.

If you're wondering what becomes of Palamon, Arcite, and Emily in the end, Arcite dies so Palamon gets the girl.

Bolt Upright

> Fair was this yonge wyf, and therewithal
> As any wezele hir body gent and smal....
> Hir mouth was sweete as bragot or the meeth,
> Or hoord of apples leyd in hey or heeth.
> Wynsynge she was, as is a joly colt,
> Long as a mast, and upright as a bolt.

> *The Canterbury Tales: The Miller's Tale,*
> A.3233–34, 3261–64

> *Fair was this young wife, and moreover*
> *Her body as delicate and small as a weasel's....*
> *Her mouth was as sweet as honeyed ale or mead,*
> *Or a hoard of apples laid in hay or heath.*
> *Skittish she was, as is a frisky colt,*
> *Long as a mast, and upright as a bolt.*

He seyde, "Thou John, thou swynes-heed, awak,
For Cristes saule, and heer a noble game.
For by that lord that called is seint Jame,
As I have thries in this shorte nyght
Swyved the milleres doghter bolt upright."

The Canterbury Tales:
The Reeve's Tale, A.4262–66

He [Allen] said, "John, you swine's-head, awake,
For Christ's soul, and hear a noble game.
For by that lord that's called Saint James,
I have thrice in this short night
Screwed the miller's daughter bolt upright."

Chaucer liked this expression so much he coined it twice, doing it better the second time. He's the first source anyone's found for either form—"upright as a bolt" or "bolt upright." You may, upon reflection, wonder what's so upright about a squat little screw, but in fact by *bolt* Chaucer means a kind of thick arrow, as used in a crossbow. In other words, "upright as a bolt" is best translated "straight as an arrow."

Bolt upright—which turns the noun into an adverb— is of course the more forcible phrasing, which is appropriate here since the Reeve's tale is an excercise in aggression. The Reeve's and Miller's stories form a pair, similar in structure and verbal crudity, each teller making a fool of the other.

The butt of the Miller's naughty narrative is an old carpenter, just like the Reeve. This fellow happened to be married to a very beautiful young woman, petite yet vigorous, tall and "upright as a bolt." (The comparison to a weasel is actually intended as flattery.) Naturally, as always happens in this sort of story, the young wife is eventually smitten by a young man, and together they pull the wool over the old fool's eyes.

To Wet One's Whistle

Wel hath this millere vernysshed his heed;
Ful pale he was for dronken, and nat reed.
He yexeth, and he speketh thurgh the nose
As he were on the quakke, or on the pose.
To bedde he goth, and with hym goth his wyf.
As any jay she light was and jolyf,
So was hir joly whistle wel ywet.

The Canterbury Tales:
The Reeve's Tale, A.4149–55

The miller has well shined his head;
He's so drunk that he's pale, not red.
He belches, and he speaks through the nose
As if he were croaking, or had a head cold.
To bed he goes, and with him goes his wife.
She was as light and frisky as a jay,
So well was her merry whistle wet.

Though he's a big important man now, the Reeve began his career as a carpenter. The Miller makes fun of an elderly carpenter in his tale (page 24), and this is the revenge.

The Reeve tells of a thoroughly despicable miller, a violent and greedy slob who steals from his customers. Needless to say this fellow gets what's coming to him when two Oxford clerks he's tried to swindle pay him back by sleeping with his daughter and his wife in his very own bedroom.

The immediate prelude to this episode is several rounds of good strong ale, which makes the miller sick but puts his wife in a frisky mood. Chaucer paints the picture with suitably ludicrous language. *To varnish your head,* in medieval parlance, meant "to drink till your whole head's red," though the miller varnishes so well that he's beyond red and into white. *On the quakke* means "hoarse," though not particularly in the style of a duck, since *quack* didn't refer exclusively to that fowl for several centuries.

Best of all is the Reeve's description of the miller's wife, stimulated by drink in a different way. Her *joly whistle* was *wel ywet,* to coin a phrase. The noun *whistle,* as in "shrill pipe," had been around for a while, but Chaucer is the first writer known to have used it as slang for mouth. And thus, obviously, he was the first to record the saying "wet your whistle."

As Fresh as a Rose

What eyleth yow to grucche thus and grone?
Is if for ye wolde have my queynte allone?
Wy, taak it al! lo, have it every deel!
Peter! I shrewe yow, but ye love it weel;
For I wolde selle my *bele chose,*
I koulde walke as fressh as is a rose;
But I wol kepe it for youre owene tooth.
Ye be to blame, by God! I sey yow sooth.

*The Canterbury Tales: The Wife of
Bath's Prologue,* D.443–50

*What ails you that you grouch thus and groan?
Is it that you would have my privates to yourself?
Why, take it all! Have the whole thing!
Saint Peter! But I swear that you love it well;
If I wanted to sell my* belle *chose,
I could walk as fresh as is a rose;
But I will keep it for your own tooth.
You're to blame, by God! And that's the truth.*

In this lengthy prologue to her tale, the Wife of Bath practically roars through what must have struck Chaucer's audience as an appalling exhibition. Not only does she boast of her career as a nagging, deceitful, and adulterous wife (five times over), but her mouth is also rather foul. *Bele chose* ("sweet thing") and especially *queynte* would not have passed in polite conversation; both refer to her private parts.

It's in the midst of this discussion with one of her husbands about how she manages her "quaint" that the wife coins "fresh as a rose." (No doubt she wasn't the first to say it, but Chaucer was the first to record it.) Having been married three times at this point, the Wife is hardly what you'd call *fresh,* at least not like a flower. She's not kidding herself, but what she does claim is that *if* she wanted to, she could make herself up to *look* fresh and virginal. She has no doubt she can put her *belle chose* back on the market whenever she likes.

While subsequent events prove her correct, the point isn't that she's right, but that she convinces her doddering spouse. This is a typical performance for the Wife: Whenever a husband catches on to her hanky-panky, she takes the offensive, denying her acts while insisting on her ability and right to do them. That way the fool is either appeased or left cowering.

The basic theme of the Wife's prologue is that, in her opinion, there's no good reason a man should have the high hand in a marriage. To her mind, marriage is a matter of power, and she doesn't hesitate to grab it when she can. When the Wife finally gets around to telling her tale, its theme is the same: What women want most is "to have sovereynetee" and "been in maistrie" over their husbands and lovers (D.1038–40).

The Wife may not be fresh as a rose, but at least she's refreshing. And Chaucer has fun deflating the idealism of such phrases, though in a more serious and innocent moment he also coins "fresh as the month of May," applied more fittingly to the Squire *(General Prologue,* A.92).

To See and Be Seen

> Myn housbonde was at Londoun al that Lente;
> I hadde the bettre leyser for to pleye,
> And for to se, and eek for to be seye
> Of lusty folk.

> *The Canterbury Tales: The Wife of*
> *Bath's Prologue, D.550–53*

> *My husband was at London all that Lent;*
> *I had the better leisure to play,*
> *And to see, and also to be seen*
> *By fun-loving folk.*

The Wife of Bath is no scholar, and her Latin is probably not very good. But whether she knows it or not, she's quoting from one of Antiquity's most notorious classics, Ovid's *Ars Amatoria* (*The Art of Love*). "*Spectatum veniunt*," wrote Ovid, "*veniunt spectentur ut ipsae*": "They come to see, and they also come to be seen."

The Wife couldn't have chosen a more apt quotation. Ovid's *Ars* is a handbook for adulterers, as shocking to his contemporaries (including Caesar Augustus) as the brazenly adulterous Wife's tale was to Chaucer's. Like the Wife, Ovid describes the provocative public displays of "lusty folk." Hot-to-trot Romans gathered at public games to see and be seen; the Wife attends the medieval equivalents: weddings, plays, preachings, processionals, and pilgrimages. She's not trekking to Canterbury for strictly religious reasons.

Her choice of the term *lusty* is also apt. In Chaucer's day the word had many meanings, including "merry" and "vigorous" as well as "lustful." Chaucer usually intends one of the first two meanings, but in the Wife's case he probably meant all three.

Though the Wife has earned a place in proverb lore as the first English translator of Ovid's line, we don't quote her verbatim. The precise expression "To see and be seen" first appears in Ben Jonson's wedding poem "Epithalamion" (1609). Then as now, weddings were more than celebrations of one pairing; they were also opportunities for new ones.

Child's Play

"I waren you wel, it is no childes pley
To take a wyf withouten avysement.
Men moste enquere, this is myn assent,
Wher she be wys, or sobre, or dronkelewe,
Or proud or elles ootehrweyes a shrewe,
A chidestere, or wastour of thy good,
Or riche, or poore, or elles mannyssh wood."

The Canterbury Tales:
The Merchant's Tale, E.1530–36

"I'm warning you, it's not child's play
To take a wife without advisement.
Men must inquire, in my opinion,
Whether she be prudent, or sober, or often drunk,
Or proud or else otherwise a shrew,
A scold, or a spendthrift,
Or rich, or poor, or mannish-mad."

What we mean by "child's play" today—something ridiculously easy—is not what Chaucer meant. In this context *no childes pley* means "not just a game"; it's a question of seriousness rather than difficulty.

In particular, it's no game to take a wife without advisement, as the speaker (Justinius) tells his brother (January). The 60-year-old January, after a long career as a rake, is finally determined to marry; and like many old fools in medieval folklore, he's determined to marry a sexy young girl. So he gathers together his friends and charges them with finding some pliant "yong flessh" to feed his desire and get him an heir.

Justinius spoils the party with serious advice. If you're going to entrust your property and body to somebody, he tells January, you'd better look into her background and character first. And one should think twice before taking a young bride; they're trouble enough for young men to keep to themselves.

Predictably, January brushes off his wiser brother's warnings. The rest of the story follows.

Love Is Blind

> But natheless, bitwixe ernest and game,
> He atte laste apoynted hym on oon,
> And leet alle othere from his herte goon,
> And chees hire of his owene auctoritee;
> For love is blynd alday, and may nat see.

> *The Canterbury Tales:*
> *The Merchant's Tale,* E.1594–98

> *Nevertheless, half in earnest and half in jest,*
> *He at last settled himself on one,*
> *And let all the others pass from his heart,*
> *And chose her on his own judgment;*
> *For love is always blind, and cannot see.*

Convinced that he knows what he's doing, the amorous old knight January (page 32) sets about choosing a fresh young wife. For a while he wavers among the town's supply, preferring one for her beauty and then another for her reputation. But in the end, not deciding so much as just stopping, he settles on a lass named May.

❧

The Merchant foreshadows the results when he moralizes redundantly that "love is blynd alday, and may nat see." January chooses May for all sorts of nice qualities, from her "armes longe and sklender" to her "wise governaunce," but some of those qualities are just his fantasies. Driven by his desire and his misplaced self-confidence, January sees (and inflates) only May's attractions, without considering her shortcomings.

January would have been wise to heed Justinius's warnings before jumping into a May/December wedding. (In Chaucer's day the year began in March, so January was late rather than early.) As predicted, he is unable to satisfy his wife, and she unable to resist temptation.

Eventually January goes literally blind and grows increasingly jealous and suspicious. But May figures out a way to foil him, even though he literally refuses to ever let go of her hand. I won't spoil the ending for you, except to say that what happens next involves one of January's servants, a pear tree, and an argument between the god Pluto and his wife Proserpina.

Chaucer can't claim to have invented the notion that "Love is blind," which traces back at least to Classical Rome. Writers including Plautus, Horace, Ovid, Propertius, and Catullus allude to "blind love," and in medieval art we find many images of little blind Cupid. But even if some similar phrase was already a cliché, Chaucer was the first to get an English version on paper (or parchment).

The notion of a May/January (or May/December) wedding also seems to trace to *The Merchant's Tale,* which unlike most others has no direct model. As noted above, January was at the time very late in the year, and thus May even earlier; but January or December, the idea's the same: the marriage of a man in his winter years with a maid in her spring is unnatural and probably doomed. December replaced January around the turn of the 17th century, exactly as England was switching to the new calendar, which made January the new first month.

As Busy as a Bee

"Ey! Goddes mercy!" seyde oure Hooste tho,
"Now swich a wyf I pray God kepe me fro!
Lo, whiche sleightes and subtilitees
In wommen been! for ay as bisy as bees
Been they, us sely men for to deceyve,
And from the soothe evere wol they weyve;
By this Marchauntes tale it preveth weel."

The Canterbury Tales:
The Merchant's Tale, E.2419–25

"Ah! God's mercy!" our Host said then,
"Now I pray God keep me from such a wife!
Lo, what devices and tricks
There are in women! for truly as busy as bees
They are to deceive us simple men,
And from the truth ever will they stray;
This Merchant's tale certainly proves that."

The Host obviously didn't need much convincing if he thinks the Merchant's tale of January and May "proves" that women are always scheming to deceive their mates. You could say, based on surviving texts, that Chaucer's whole culture was prepared to believe the slur; but then that would just be repeating the Host's mistake—generalizing facts from fictions.

～✦～

Chaucer's having some fun at the Host's expense here, though it isn't the first time his fun involved unflattering female stereotypes. Take *Troilus and Criseyde,* for another example. According to Chaucer, the god of Love, enraged at his portrait of an immoral, conniving woman, demanded that he compensate by writing *The Legend of Good Women*. Not that its portraits of literal or figurative saints is any more realistic.

Actually, to call women "*bisy as bees*" is not such an insult, though you do have to extricate it from context. Since Classical times bees were symbols of tireless industry, nature's own role models. You might suspect that the Host has in mind the negative sense of *busy* (as in *busybody*), which would echo his imputations of sleights, subtleties, and deceptions; but that sense postdates *The Canterbury Tales.*

Patience Is a Virtue

> Wommen, of kynde, desiren libertee,
> And nat to been constreyned as a thral;
> And so doon men, if I sooth seyen shal.
> Looke who that is moost pacient in love,
> He is at his avantage al above.
> Pacience is an heigh vertu, certeyn,
> For it vanquysseth, as thise clerkes seyn,
> Thynges that rigour sholde nevere atteyne.

The Canterbury Tales:
The Franklin's Tale, F.768–75

Women by nature desire liberty,
And not to be held in thrall;
And so do men, to tell the truth.
Observe who is most patient in love,
He has the advantage over all.
Patience is a high virtue, indeed,
For as the clerks say, it conquers
Things that severity should never attain.

The Franklin's Tale is last in what scholars call the "marriage group," which began with the Wife of Bath's tale, and which offers a wide variety of tips and advice. The Franklin presents his main point here: Women, like men, resent being lorded over and treated harshly. The secret to a peaceful and happy marriage is mutual patience.

Once again, Chaucer molds an old idea into its characteristic English form, give or take a qualifier. His model may have been the Classical adage *vincit qui patitur*—"He who is patient [or who suffers] overcomes," which is the Franklin's main thesis. In praising virtue for its own sake he was more directly anticipated by Langland, who wrote in *Piers Plowman* that "Suffraunce is a sovereygne vertue." But Chaucer was the first to put patience in the phrase.

The Franklin goes on to demonstrate the virtues of patience and mutual respect with the moving tale of a faithful wife and an understanding husband. It's one of the very few *Canterbury Tales* in which everybody ends up looking good.

∽✦∽

Murder Will Out

> I seye that in a wardrobe they hym threwe
> Where as thise Jewes purgen hire entraille.
> O cursed folk of Herodes al newe,
> What may youre yvel entente yow availle?
> Mordre wol out, certeyn, it wol nat faille,
> And namely ther th'onour of God shal sprede;
> The blood out crieth on youre cursed dede.

> *The Canterbury Tales:*
> *The Prioress's Tale, B.1762–68*

> *I say that they threw him in a cesspit*
> *Where these Jews purged their bowels.*
> *O cursed modern people of Herod,*
> *What good will your evil designs do you?*
> *Murder will out, certainly, it will not fail,*
> *Especially where the honor of God shall spread;*
> *The blood cries out on your cursed deed.*

This vile little tale, courtesy of the holy and delicate Prioress, is the most striking demonstration of Chaucer's willingness and ability to mirror even the ugliest attitudes of his age.

The hero of the story, which is set in some Asian city, is a devout Christian innocent, a schoolboy merely seven years old. The villains are the city's usurious Jews, "Hateful to Crist," depicted as latter-day followers of Herod, which is to say would-be Christ-killers. (Medieval Christians were especially ready to confuse the Jews with their erstwhile Roman governors.)

According to the Prioress, the schoolboy's pure and total devotion to the Virgin Mary so enrages Satan that he stirs up the Jewish ghetto to murder him. A hired assassin cuts the boy's throat and throws him into a *wardrobe,* or cesspit. What they don't know, and what will spell their doom, is that "*Mordre wol out*": So evil a deed cannot be hid.

What the Prioress means by "murder will out" is of course that "murder will come out." The expression is actually a little odd, requiring either that *will* mean "will be forced" or that *out* mean "come out." The former may seem more natural, but both are possible because *out* was once commonly used as a verb, meaning "to exhibit" or "to eject." In which case the Prioress should have said "murder will be outed." If she had she would have coined another modern expression.

To Stink Like a Goat

And everemoore, where that evere they goon,
Men may hem knowe by smel of brymstoon.
For al the world they stynken as a goot;
Hir savour is so rammyssh and so hoot
That though a man from hem a mile be,
The savour wole infecte hym, trusteth me.

The Canterbury Tales:
The Canon's Yeoman's Tale, G.884–89

And always, wherever they go,
Men may know them by smell of brimstone.
For all the world they stink like a goat;
Their smell is so rammish and so strong
That though a man be a mile away,
The smell will infect him, trust me.

✑

Men never tire of looking to get something for nothing. Today we go for sweepstakes, pyramid schemes, and IPOs; in Chaucer's time the scam was alchemy. The Canon's Yeoman exposes all the tricks, blithely blabbing on his boss the Canon, who slinks off when he sees where the Yeoman is going.

If you're looking for an alchemist, the Yeoman says, you won't have much trouble. They spend all day and all night cooking up rank mixtures of stuff like *brymstoon* (sulphur), and thus they "stink like a goat." Their aroma is so potent that it will knock you out a mile away.

It doesn't profit them much, either, even counting the money they extract from gullible patrons. Anything valuable they produce with their hocus-pocus is more than eaten up by the cost of materials. So why bother, and why put up with the stench? Because though many alchemists were con artists, even some of those actually believed (or hoped) they could find some method of turning base metals into gold. However deluded, these alchemists did ultimately contribute something to society: They invented chemistry.

❧

All That Glitters Is Not Gold

> Allas! what harm doth apparence,
> Whan hit is fals in existence!
> For he to hir a traytour was;
> Wherfore she slow hirself, allas!
> Loo, how a woman doth amys
> To love him that unknowen ys!
> For, be Cryste, lo, thus yt fareth:
> "Hyt is not al gold that glareth."

> *The House of Fame* (ca. 1375),
> Book I, 265–72

> *Alas! what harm appearance does,*
> *When it is false in reality!*
> *For he was a traitor to her;*
> *Wherefore she slew herself, alas!*
> *Lo, how a woman does amiss*
> *To love him that is unknown!*
> *For, by Christ, lo, thus it goes:*
> *"All that glitters is not gold."*

One of the morals of the *Canon's Yeoman's Tale* (page 39) is that what appears precious is often not, or as the Yeoman puts it, "al thyng which that shineth as the gold / Nis nat gold" (G.962–63). Chaucer had used a similar phrase earlier in his career, in this passage from *The House of Fame,* a dream-vision of famous love stories.

One of the most famous was the tragic tale of Dido and Aeneas, as told by Virgil in the *Aeneid.* According to Virgil, Aeneas, a Trojan prince, flees Troy as the Greeks burn it down and sets off in search of a new home. Along the way, having lost his wife somewhere, he makes a stop in

Carthage, where he captures the heart of Queen Dido. Once he's got her hooked, though, he bolts; we can't entirely blame him, because the gods make him do it. Nonetheless, the heartbroken queen throws herself into a fire.

Chaucer isn't so forgiving, and he milks the pathos here. Aeneas is a *traytour,* a man who only *seems* noble and true, and he's not alone among the male sex. Seeming dreamboats are often scoundrels, and women are forewarned not to fall in love with men they don't know. He caps the warning with the quotable line, "Hyt is not al gold that glareth."

It's so quotable that he puts the phrase in quotation marks, though we know of no earlier English version. Chaucer may be referring to a proverb his audience would have known in Latin—such a phrase has been found, but only in manuscripts later than Chaucer's. In any case, Chaucer says *glareth* rather than *glittereth.* The latter term first appears, with an alternate spelling, in the Renaissance proverb, "All that glisters is not gold."

To Strike While the Iron Is Hot

> Pandare, which that stood hire faste by,
> Felt iren hoot, and he bygan to smyte,
> And seyde, "Nece, I pray you heartely,
> Telle me that I shal axen you a lite."

> *Troilus and Criseyde* (ca. 1385),
> Book II, 1275–78

> *Pandarus, who stood right by her,*
> *Felt the iron hot, and he began to smite,*

And said, "Niece, I pray you heartily,
Tell me a little what I ask."

Of the three main figures in Chaucer's *Troilus and Criseyde*—the title pair plus Pandarus—only Troilus has escaped becoming an insult. Chaucer is less to blame here than his predecessor (and source) Boccaccio, whose version is rather more cynical than Chaucer's.

In outline, though, their tales are the same. The action takes place in Troy during the war with Greece. Cressida's father, Calchas, has turned traitor and joined with the Greeks, leaving behind his daughter and her uncle Pandarus. Cressida begins to fancy the Trojan prince Troilus, and he her, and Pandarus orchestrates a secret affair. But faithful Troilus is betrayed by false Cressida, who's sent to Greece in an exchange of prisoners and who begins a new affair there with the Greek prince Diomedes.

Since Cressida's betrayal was first told in an old French romance, she has symbolized the weak and faithless lover. And since Boccaccio introduced the scheming Pandaro, he has stood for the unscrupulous middleman. In later English a *pandar* was a pimp. In *Hamlet* Shakespeare turned the noun into a verb meaning "to shamelessly serve another's desires." The meaning of *pander* today is less strong but still negative: "to give the people what they want."

But Chaucer's Pandarus, though a man of the world, means no harm—after all, he's Criseyde's uncle and Troilus's friend. But his exertions are mysteriously strenuous, and his methods a bit manipulative. In this passage, for example, he stands with Criseyde as they watch Troilus ride by, and notices her turn "red as rose" and show other signs of being smitten. The *iren,* so to speak, is *hoot,* and Pandarus does some smiting of his own, prying through

Criseyde's weak defenses to get her to admit to her lust. (Chaucer takes the metaphor from a blacksmith's shop.)

Outside the *Canterbury Tales,* where it appears twice, the coinage shows up only once again before the 16th century, in the *Troy-book* (1420) of Chaucer's sincerest admirer, John Lydgate. (Lydgate quotes the *Troilus* version word for word.) Sometime before the publication of John Heywood's *Proverbs* in 1546, the phrase took on its modern form, which Heywood gives as "When thy iron is hot, strike." The verb was put first by 1587.

To Let Sleeping Dogs Lie

> "It is nought good a slepyng hound to wake,
> Ne yeve a wight a cause to devyne."
>
> *Troilus and Criseyde,* Book III, 764–65

> *"It is not good to wake a sleeping dog,*
> *Nor give a person a cause to suspect."*

This coinage is based on a 13th-century French proverb, *Il fait mal éveiller le chien qui dort:* "It's bad to wake the dog that sleeps." Chaucer, the first to say so in English, got the French right, but his version didn't last. Sir Walter Scott put it the way we remember in *Redgauntlet* (1824): "Best to let sleeping dogs lie."

In this particular instance, Pandarus is warning Criseyde to hold her tongue. He's just crept into her bedchamber—one of Pandarus's guest rooms—through a trap door, sending the alarmed Criseyde into a fit. He stops her before she cries out, an act he's sure would give the servants cause for unfounded suspicion.

Actually, this creepy episode does put Pandarus in a bad light. Unbeknownst to Criseyde, he's brought Troilus home, and is arranging to get him into her bed. Pandarus lies and cajoles and practically forces the two together, though in the end they have a good time.

In One Ear and Out the Other

Thise wordes seyde he for the nones alle,
To help his frend, lest he for sorwe deyde;
For douteles, to don his wo to falle,
He roughte nought what unthrift that he seyde.
But Troilus, that neigh for sorwe deyde,
Took litel heede of al that evere he mente;
Oon ere it herde, at tothir out it wente.

Troilus and Criseyde, Book IV, 428–34

[Pandarus] said these words in order
To help his friend, lest he die for sorrow;
In fact, to decrease [Troilus's] woe,
He didn't care what foolishness he said.
But Troilus, who was close to dying for sorrow,
Took little heed of anything he said;
One ear heard it, and out the other it went.

Literary history clearly proves that this phrase descends directly from Chaucer. His distinctive contraction of *the othir* to *tothir* is preserved in written quotations for at least 400 years; for example, Jonathan Swift wrote in 1738 that "All they can say goes in at one ear and out at t'other for me."

The meaning, of course, is that one's brain can't process the incoming data, either because it's preoccupied or (as in this case) numb. Both Pandarus and Troilus have just heard the news that Criseyde is to be traded to Greece for a Trojan prisoner named Antenor, and both practically lose their minds.

Pandarus manages to get a grip on himself, and he rushes to his friend's chamber to deliver the usual feckless cheer for the heartbroken. This town's full of women better than Criseyde, he says, and I'll arrange a new match with one of them. Besides, you got to spend the night with her, which is more than I can say.

This is the sort of thing that goes in one of Troilus's ears and out the other. Even Pandarus knows it's no good, but he'll say any foolish thing if there's a chance it will rouse Troilus from his self-pity. Eventually Troilus does reply, vowing that he will never look at another woman, which would be treason to her "that trewe is unto me." Chaucer probably means this to increase our pity for

Troilus—we all know Criseyde will betray him; but it also makes Troilus look pretty naive.

To Make a Virtue of Necessity

"And forthi sle with resoun al this hete!
Men seyn, 'the suffrant overcomith,' parde;
Ek 'whoso wol han lief, he lief moot lete.'
Thus maketh vertu of necessite
By pacience, and thynk that lord is he
Of Fortune ay, that naught wole of hire recche;
And she ne daunteth no wight but a wrecche."

Troilus and Criseyde, Book IV, 1583–89

"And therefore slay all this heat with reason!
Men say, 'the patient man triumphs,' to be sure;
And 'whoever would love, he must give up love.'
Thus make a virtue of necessity
By patience, and think that he is the lord
Of fortune, aye, that takes no notice of her;
And she daunts no man but a wretch."

In the last conversation Criseyde will ever have with Troilus, she cautions him against acting like too big a fool. Their forced separation is awful, of course; and it's too bad that she's going to live in the enemy camp. But in the event of peace they can pick up where they left off. And if Troilus makes too big a deal out of her leaving, their secret will be revealed; he'll look like a crybaby, and her honor will be spotted with "filthe."

Be reasonable, she pleads with him here; cool down and learn to be patient, for patience overcomes (compare "Patience Is a Virtue," page 36). To grasp after love is no way to attain it; you must be willing to lose it all. Fortune smiles on those who pay her no mind, not on those who debase themselves for her.

To extract the key line from this sermon, "Thus maketh vertu of necessite/ By pacience." There's nothing he can do about her going to the Greeks, so he may as well handle the situation with virtue and dignity. The "necessity" of loss, she says, will actually teach him valuable lessons on patience. As when people trot out this proverb today, it sounds a little condescending.

Chaucer adapted the saying from similar expressions in Latin and French literature; a version appears in the *Roman de la Rose,* which he had partly translated earlier in his career. The slightly modified modern version, "to make a virtue of necessity," first appears in Shakespeare's *Two Gentlemen of Verona.*

William Shakespeare

William Shakespeare (1564–1616), the greatest poet in history, wrote little poetry outside his drama. There, he excelled in blank verse, though his facility with rhyme was also considerable (see *A Midsummer Night's Dream*). He had little interest in any other sort of poetic career; the theater was his business as well as his art.

What other verse Shakespeare composed, including his sonnets of the 1590s, he wrote in his minimal spare time, or whenever a plague broke out and shut the theaters. Most of this nondramatic poetry, including a good half of the sonnets, pales in comparison to the plays.

Make no mistake: Shakespeare's sonnets are, on the whole, wonderful. But he'd hardly be worshipped as he is on their basis alone. He could do amazing things in fourteen lines, but those confines were too small and too contrived for his gifts. The sonnet form was well suited to the sensibility and tastes of Shakespeare's age; by the same token, his accomplishments there were more for his age than for all time.

Nonetheless, out of the 154 sonnets attributed to Shakespeare, at least several dozen are so deep, intense, and beautiful that they continue to be read and remembered. Here are ten of those we remember best.

Shall I Compare Thee to a Summer's Day?

Shall I compare thee to a summer's day?
Thou art more lovely and more temperate:
Rough winds do shake the darling buds of May,
And summer's lease hath all too short a date;
Sometime too hot the eye of heaven shines,
And often is his gold complexion dimmed;
And every fair from fair sometime declines,
By chance of nature's changing course
    untrimmed:
But thy eternal summer shall not fade,
Nor lose possession of that fair thou ow'st,
Nor shall death brag thou wand'rest in his shade,
When in eternal lines to time thou grow'st.
  So long as men can breathe or eyes can see,
  So long lives this, and this gives life to thee.

Sonnet 18

If you thought Shakespeare was comparing a summer's day to some fair young maid who captured his heart, you were wrong. Rather, his object is a comely young nobleman dear to his heart. Like most of the sonnets, this one is probably semi-autobiographical, though who the "Young Man" really was has been a question subjected to centuries of tireless and ultimately senseless debate.

Sonnet 18 is one of a large group of boldly flattering tributes to the boy, whom the poet claims is better than a summer's day. Actually, what he means is better than your *average* summer day, which isn't always all that nice—summer has hot days, and overcast days, and other less-than-perfect days. (The winds of May get thrown in for good measure.) In contrast, the Young Man is always nice, always lovely and temperate, his complexion always exquisite.

Granting Shakespeare his right to hyperbole, you can sort of follow the argument so far. Things grow more dubious, though, as the poet proceeds. He points out that even when it's good, summer must come to an end; surely he isn't implying that the Young Man won't?

In a way, that's exactly what he means. Obviously the flesh-and-blood specimen will eventually lose some of his luster; nor can he avoid the *shade* (shadow) of death. But the man will remain young in the "eternal summer" of poetry. That is, Shakespeare has enshrined his perfection in the sonnets, and the sonnets will be read "So long as men can breathe or eyes can see."

Shakespeare wasn't the first or last to boast this way in a sonnet, but even so the boast is amazingly arrogant. On the other hand, it's probably true.

When in Disgrace with Fortune and Men's Eyes...

When in disgrace with fortune and men's eyes
I all alone beweep my outcast state,
And trouble deaf heav'n with my bootless cries,
And look upon myself and curse my fate,
Wishing me like to one more rich in hope,
Featured like him, like him with friends pos-
    sessed,
Desiring this man's art, and that man's scope,
With what I most enjoy contented least;
Yet in these thoughts myself almost despising,
Haply I think on thee, and then my state,
Like to the lark at break of day arising
From sullen earth, sings hymns at heaven's gate;
    For thy sweet love rememb'red such wealth
        brings,
    That then I scorn to change my state with
        kings.

Sonnet 29

This sonnet certainly gets off to a fine start—literarily, that is—with one of Shakespeare's most memorable lines. The content isn't so happy. "When in disgrace with fortune and men's eyes" means "When down on my luck and shunned by all," and this is just the beginning of Shakespeare's pity party.

He goes on to moan about his loneliness and grief, heaven's indifference to his cries, his lack of "friends" (benefactors), his anger and self-loathing, his insecurity and dissatisfaction, and so on. Yet there's a turn at line 9, when, on the brink of despair, the poet "haply" ("by chance," but also "happily") thinks of his beloved Young Man. Suddenly the sun is shining and all's right with the world.

You may be wondering at this point exactly what sort of relationship the poet has with the youth whose "sweet love" lifts his soul to "heaven's gate." Not to disappoint you, but the affair was entirely platonic, though at times the poet expresses interesting opinions about it. Take Sonnet 20, in which Shakespeare imagines that the Young Man was originally created woman, before doting Nature (a female) added "one thing to my purpose nothing."

Remembrance of Things Past

When to the sessions of sweet silent thought
I summon up remembrance of things past,
I sigh the lack of many a thing I sought,
And with old woes new wail my dear time's
    waste.
Then can I drown an eye, unused to flow,
For precious friends hid in death's dateless night,
And weep afresh love's long since canceled woe,
And moan th' expense of many a vanished sight.
Then can I grieve at grievances foregone,
And heavily from woe to woe tell o'er
The sad account of fore-bemoanèd moan,
Which I new pay as if not paid before.
    But if the while I think on thee, dear friend,
    All losses are restored, and sorrows end.

Sonnet 30

This is basically Sonnet 29, Take Two, only the misfortune here is past and the salvation reduced to a couplet. In the previous poem (page 52), the poet was describing new disgraces and disappointments; here, he only remembers them, but in the memory experiences them anew. And once again, thoughts of his beloved Young Man put an end to his weeping.

Truth be told, the first poem is better. But the second verse of this one is far better known, though it's associated more with Marcel Proust than with Shakespeare. The original French title of Proust's gargantuan seven-volume novel was *À la recherche du temps perdu,* literally *In Search of Lost Time.* But Proust's original English translator, C. K. Scott Moncrieff, found the bare translation too uninspiring, and so he turned to the Bard, always a gold mine for titles.

Proust's novel benefited from the borrowing; the sonnet has not. "Remembrance of things past" has since devolved into a kind of "classy" brand name for sentimental commemorative volumes and nostalgic memoirs.

Another literary note: By *foregone* in line 9 Shakespeare means "gone before." The word is never used today except in the phrase "foregone conclusion," which Shakespeare coined in *Othello* (1604).

Gilded Monuments

Not marble nor the gilded monuments
Of princes shall outlive this pow'rful rhyme,
But you shall shine more bright in these contents
Than unswept stone, besmeared with sluttish time.
When wasteful war shall statues overturn,

And broils root out the work of masonry,
Nor Mars his sword nor war's quick fire shall burn
The living record of your memory.
'Gainst death and all obvious enmity
Shall you pace forth; your praise shall still find
    room,
Ev'n in the eyes of all posterity
That wear this world out to the ending doom.
  So, till the judgment that yourself arise,
   You live in this, and dwell in lovers' eyes.

Sonnet 55

Continuing the theme of Sonnet 18 (page 50), Shakespeare once again insists that his poems grant their subject, the Young Man, immortality.

Immortality was precisely the poet's rationale in the earliest sonnets for urging the youth to marry and procreate. Later he drops that theme to promise eternal youth in verse. By the 55th sonnet the tune is beginning to sour; you wouldn't exactly call it a happy poem.

In the "summer's day" poem, death makes a brief and rather delicate appearance. Here the tone is much more brutal, the threats more stark: "sluttish time," "wasteful war," "oblivious enmity," "the ending doom." Not to mention *broils* (tumults), the sword of Mars (the Roman war god), and other forms of riot and destruction.

No matter: Shakespeare's poetry is stronger. It will live on in the "eyes of all posterity," longer even than marble or all the "gilded monuments" powerful men erect to their memory. The rages of war can destroy any stone, or the strongest of structures, but they can't destroy a poem.

Well, so what? Neither, by the same logic, could war destroy *Mutant Message from Down Under.* Shakespeare makes much of his poetry's permanence, but the real point is what he thinks it will last to do. Shakespeare isn't just preserving the memory of a very special young man, but also through writing preserving the spirit of his love. It's this love that he wants to pass on, keeping it alive in "lovers' eyes."

The Marriage of True Minds

Let me not to the marriage of true minds
Admit impediments. Love is not love
Which alters when it alteration finds,
Or bends with the remover to remove.
O no, it is an ever-fixèd mark
That looks on tempests and is never shaken;
It is the star to every wand'ring bark,
Whose worth's unknown, although his height be
    taken.
Love's not time's fool, though rosy lips and cheeks
With his bending sickle's compass come.
Love alters not with his brief hours and weeks,
But bears it out ev'n to the edge of doom.
    If this be error and upon me proved,
    I never writ, nor no man ever loved.

Sonnet 116

"The marriage of true minds" is a phrase both widely quoted and difficult to grasp, at least in the way Shakespeare meant it. By speaking more briefly of a "marriage of the minds," we manage to avoid the issue of what "true" means, though it's essential to the point of the poem.

We apply the phrase to compatible intellects, and that's certainly part of what Shakespeare meant. But in the poem *marriage* isn't so abstract: it comes closer to a literal marriage, being a total relationship, mind plus body. So *true minds* doesn't mean "authentic minds" or even "great minds," but "faithful spirits." In Shakespeare's day, *truth* had "fidelity" as one of its primary senses.

If you follow this point, you can see how Shakespeare gets on to the topic of constancy in love. Love isn't really love at all, he says, if it bends under circumstance or alters as the world does. Love isn't an affair of convenience, subject to whim, but resolute like an "ever-fixèd mark." (*Mark* refers to a stationary object on land or sea used as a reference in navigating.) Nor is true love dependent on transitory things such as youth or beauty. It weathers all tempests and remains unmoved.

The payoff of love is this very stability. Since human beings are by nature fickle and foolish, they require a navigator, a guiding force to keep them out of trouble. By portraying true love as this force, Shakespeare separates love from lovers, as if it could exist without them. Philosophers call this a "Platonic ideal." The only problem with Platonic ideals is that reality can never compete.

'Tis Better to Be Vile Than Vile Esteemed...

'Tis better to be vile than vile esteemed,
When not to be receives reproach of being,
And the just pleasure lost, which is so deemed,

Not by our feeling but by others' seeing.
For why should others' false adulterate eyes
Give salutation to my sportive blood?
Or on my frailties why are frailer spies,
Which in their wills count bad what I think good?
No, I am that I am, and they that level
At my abuses reckon up their own;
I may be straight though they themselves be bevel.
By their rank thoughts my deeds must not be
    shown,
  Unless this general evil they maintain—
  All men are bad and in their badness reign.

                     Sonnet 121

English poets before Shakespeare had written "Shake-spearean" sonnets, but Shakespeare still got the patent. He wrote them well, which helped, but he also most brilliantly exploited their structure. Composed of three quatrains and a couplet, his sonnets slowly build and then turn, probing theses and then giving them a witty concluding twist.

Sonnet 121 is a striking example of this technique. Its theme is a variation on the cliché that "Beauty is in the eye of the beholder"; the same, Shakespeare claims, goes for ugliness. What the first two lines mean is that it's better to actually *be* wicked than to be *thought* wicked, if the good are called wicked anyway. What the poet feels is a "just pleasure" (namely, an extramarital affair) is condemned by others as "vile," but who's really the proper judge? What is the difference between seeming vile and being vile?

The poem thus raises the age-old conflict between appearance and essence, seeming and being. As far as the poet is concerned, he has every right to indulge his "sportive blood" (frisky feelings) if his conscience lets him; the urges, after all, are natural. Those who condemn him call his deeds vile not because they "really" are, but because their judgments are twisted. Even what's perfectly straight looks crooked in beveled glass.

Shakespeare boils it all down in the couplet. The thesis so far is that people, in judging us, do so from their own feelings rather than from ours; thus if they judge us evil (*vile*'s anagram), the evil really resides in them, not in us. To deny this, they must resort to *another* evil claim: that their sanctimonious judgments are absolute. But if the poet's arrogant critics really applied the same standards to everyone, we'd *all* be judged vile. This includes the critics themselves, which brings us back to the beginning, because if they're vile they can't justify their judgments of others. Aren't paradoxes fun?

Th' Expense of Spirit in a Waste of Shame…

> Th' expense of spirit in a waste of shame
> Is lust in action, and till action lust
> Is perjured, murderous, bloody, full of blame,
> Savage, extreme, rude, cruel, not to trust,
> Enjoyed no sooner but despisèd straight,
> Past reason hunted, and no sooner had,
> Past reason hated as a swallowed bait,
> On purpose laid to make the taker mad;
> Mad in pursuit, and in possession so,
> Had, having, and in quest to have, extreme,
> A bliss in proof, and proved, a very woe,
> Before, a joy proposed, behind, a dream.
> > All this the world well knows, yet none knows well
> > To shun the heav'n that leads men to this hell.

Sonnet 129

The sonnet in a nutshell: Lust is a frenzy that drives men into shameful actions. As Shakespeare admits in line 13, this isn't exactly news; but why, he asks in line 14, do we give in to it anyway?

The poem analyzes lust in its "before" and "after" phases, both of which are bad, though the brief intermission is bliss. Before we act on it, lust is ruthless, irrational, and extreme, leading to all sorts of excesses if not literally to perjury and murder. After we act on it, our spirit is drained and we sink into a shameful desolation. (Shakespeare puns naughtily in line 1: *spirit* was a euphemism for "semen.") What we were once mad to possess becomes "a very woe."

Shakespeare would treat the theme of desire's turning to disgust more fully in his tragicomedy *Troilus and Cressida* (1602). There are many lines in the play on the dangers of excess desire; Ulysses, for example, calls the lust for power a "universal wolf" which will eventually "eat himself up." About a hundred lines earlier, Cressida gives a famous speech on how much better things look before we get them:

> Women are angels, wooing:
> Things won are done; joy's soul lies in the doing.
> That she belov'd knows nought that knows not
>   this:
> Men prize the thing ungained more than it is.

In other words, women look great to a man in lust—in fact, they look much better than they really are. After they're won, however, they're more or less chopped liver. This is Cressida's explanation for keeping Troilus at arm's length—or rather, as it turns out, at finger's length.

My Mistress' Eyes Are Nothing like the Sun...

> My mistress' eyes are nothing like the sun;
> Coral is far more red than her lips' red;
> If snow be white, why then her breasts are dun;
> If hairs be wires, black wires grow on her head:
> I have seen roses damasked, red and white,
> But no such roses see I in her cheeks,

And in some perfumes is there more delight
Than in the breath that from my mistress reeks.
I love to hear her speak, yet well I know
That music hath a far more pleasing sound.
I grant I never saw a goddess go;
My mistress when she walks treads on the
    ground.
    And yet by heav'n I think my love as rare
    As any she belied with false compare.

Sonnet 130

This poem is an amusing parody of your typical sonnet in praise of a lady's excellence. And perhaps not coincidentally, it echoes one of Shakespeare's own efforts in the form, his tribute in Sonnet 18 to a young man more glorious than a summer's day (page 50).

Shakespeare's tributary here has been dubbed the "Dark Lady," an allusion to her complexion as well as her temperament. It's true that, according to the sonnets, she was rather troublesome; but, while "dark" (an opposite of *fair*), she certainly wasn't ugly. By negatively comparing her to clichés of beauty such as the sun, coral, snow, roses, and so on, Shakespeare's merely admitting that her beauty is human, not heavenly.

You may find it hard to believe that

Shakespeare isn't totally dissing the Dark Lady here, but that's an illusion due to shifting meanings. Comparing hair to wires was a compliment, because back then *wire* usually meant "fine thread of precious metal." The worst Shakespeare's saying is that her hair is black. *Reeks* is another word grown more negative with time; it didn't mean "to stink" until the 18th century—here it just means "exhales."

The last two lines, as usual, say it all. Though the lady fails to meet the ridiculous standards of poetry, it's those standards, not she, which suffer by comparison. No woman could match poetic hyperbole, which amounts to "false compare" (inaccurate if not insincere analogy). That the Dark Lady falls short of these standards—and still inspires a *rare* (uncommon and precious) love—reveals the standards as lies.

Two Loves I Have of Comfort and Despair...

Two loves I have of comfort and despair,
Which like two spirits do suggest me still;
The better angel is a man right fair,
The worser spirit a woman coloured ill.
To win me soon to hell, my female evil
Tempteth my better angel from my side,
And would corrupt my saint to be a devil,
Wooing his purity with her foul pride.
And, whether that my angel be turn'd fiend,
Suspect I may, yet not directly tell,
But being both from me, both to each friend,

I guess one angel in another's hell.
    Yet this shall I ne'er know, but live in doubt,
    Till my bad angel fire my good one out.

Sonnet 144

It's poems like these that make the later sonnets a Renaissance soap opera, the mysterious and tragicomic tale of a famous love triangle.

One player is the poet, who may or may not reveal Shakespeare's true feelings; the other two are the Young Man and the Dark Lady, whose true identities are unknown, and who may not have existed at all. It's possible Shakespeare just made the whole thing up, though that's unlikely—sonnets like this are full of oblique references and inside jokes that could only have been aimed at real persons. In other words, it's hard to figure out exactly what's going on.

This much we know: The poet has two "loves," one good and one bad, sort of like the little angel and devil who whisper in either ear. The dark bad one ("of despair") is making a play for the fair good one ("of comfort"); the poet isn't sure if she's winning, but the suspense is driving him mad. At the very least, she's spoiled their male bonding.

So far, so good (or so bad). But the last four lines are devilishly hard to untangle, even with a scorecard. Here's one reading: Because both angels are "from" the poet (not calling him), and because they're each other's friend as well as his, chances are they're out of touch for good reason. And that reason, the poet guesses, is that the good angel has turned fiend and is doing naughty things with the bad angel in her little hell. But he won't know for sure until she "fires him out," whatever that means. It might simply signify "sends him packing," but it could also mean "gives him a burning disease."

Black as Hell, Dark as Night

My love is as a fever, longing still
For that which longer nurseth the disease,
Feeding on that which doth preserve the ill,
Th' uncertain sickly appetite to please.
My reason, the physician to my love,
Angry that his prescriptions are not kept,
Hath left me, and I desp'rate now approve
Desire is death, which physic did except.
Past cure I am, now reason is past care,
And frantic mad with evermore unrest,
My thoughts and my discourse as madmen's are,
At random from the truth vainly expressed;
   For I have sworn thee fair, and thought thee
     bright,
   Who art as black as hell, as dark as night.

Sonnet 147

In his later, unhappier sonnets, Shakespeare's discourse does indeed seem mad, or at least convoluted; it has a feverish impulsiveness that's hard to follow. But at the same time they're logically rigorous and rich in meaning—there's definitely method in the madness. Such tightly controlled depictions of loss of control, which are at the same time emotionally disjointed logical exercises, are trademark Shakespeare.

The source of his eloquent "disease" is the lady we met under happier circumstances in Sonnet 130 (page 62), where the poet "swore her fair." Subsequent events have changed his mind. Once he praised her dark beauty; all that's left now is the darkness—"as black as hell, as dark as night."

Unfortunately, although he knows she's evil he still can't shake his longing, which grips him like a fever. In his sickness he craves the very thing that makes him ill, despite the better advice of Dr. Reason. By this point the doctor has thrown up his hands, abandoning the poet to his disease. His reason gone, the poet succumbs entirely to the desire that reason "did except" (forbade), and which could prove emotionally fatal ("Desire is death").

The whole poem grapples with the irony of deadly desire, the longing for that which destroys us. This contradiction is played out in the couplet, where the poet is trapped between what he feels and what he knows: The lady's seeming fairness and brightness draw him into her blackness and darkness. "Black as hell" isn't Shakespeare's coinage—it was proverbial; but the chilling conjunction with "dark as night" is his.

The Renaissance

In Shakespeare's sonnets alone the English Renaissance boasts some of the greatest poems ever written. The combined output of Shakespeare, John Donne, and John Milton make it the greatest age of English poetry. And there's lots more, some of it nearly as great as the work of those three giants. The enormous energy, innovation, depth, beauty, and quantity of English Renaissance poetry place it beyond compare.

Many different factors made the 16th and 17th centuries a fertile time for imaginative literature. It was an expansive age of great geographic and scientific discoveries, but also a time in which the Classical culture of Greece and Rome was rediscovered and embraced. All sorts of ideas, new and old, were explored with great invention and energy, and an exciting new sense of human possibilities emerged. The spread of Protestantism in England fostered a more introspective spiritual life, and poets began developing a new language of the soul. Meanwhile, the emergence of capitalism fueled unprecedented social mobility and gave people the chance to experiment with new social roles. All the (Western) world was a stage, and there's drama everywhere in Renaissance literature, even in lyric poetry.

A rising tide lifts all boats, and the genius of the age shines through in its lesser as well as its greater works. In this chapter I touch on a range of Renaissance poetry, from the merely interesting to the immortal. Authors include:

JOHN SKELTON (CA. 1460–1529): scholar and priest, tutor to Prince Henry, later the Eighth; sharp-tongued and indiscreet, he lampooned enemies in a choppy, multi-rhymed verse form dubbed "Skeltonics";

SIR THOMAS WYATT (1503–1542): a courtier who more than once found himself afoul of King Henry; a pioneer of English verse who, along with Henry Howard, Earl of Surrey, created the taste for lyric poetry;

EDMUND SPENSER (1552–1599): a government employee posted (reluctantly) for some time in Ireland; author of the elaborate and endless heroic epic *The Faerie Queene,* dedicated to Elizabeth I, and the majestic wedding-song "Epithalamion," among other works;

CHRISTOPHER MARLOWE (1564–1593): the first great dramatic poet in England, who practically invented the tragic form later perfected by Shakespeare; possibly also a spy; murdered at 29 in an argument over a bill;

JOHN DONNE (1572–1631): perhaps the greatest lyric poet in the English language; prime mover in the Metaphysical school of poetry; a libertine and a Catholic in youth but later an Anglican priest and formidable sermonizer;

BEN JONSON (1572–1637): second only to Shakespeare in comedy, Jonson was also an accomplished poet whose Classically influenced verse proved more influential than the Bard's for over a century;

ROBERT HERRICK (1591–1674): one of the "Sons of Ben," devotees and imitators of Jonson; a reluctant preacher in Devonshire who made lemonade from the lemons of country life by writing graceful lyrics on "brooks, blossoms, birds, and bowers";

RICHARD LOVELACE (1618–1657): a dashing courtier in the court of Charles I, Lovelace made enemies with Parliament and wound up twice in jail, where he wrote his best poetry;

HENRY VAUGHAN (1621–1695): another loyalist of the king's, Vaughan escaped prison but retired from public life to practice medicine in Wales; his poetry tends to the Baroque and includes references to various occult doctrines;

ANDREW MARVELL (1621–1678): friend and aid to Milton, Marvell was the next-best poet of his generation, though nobody knew it at the time; served as an M.P. from Hull after the Restoration and helped keep Milton out of jail.

A few of the many other Renaissance poets well worth reading include Sir Philip Sidney, Thomas Campion, and George Herbert.

To Keep the Wolf from the Door

How be it some there be,
Almost two or three,
Of that dignity,
Full worshipful clerks,
As appeareth by their works,
Like Aaron and Ure,
The wolf from the door
To werryn and to keep
From their ghostly sheep,
And their spiritual lambs
Sequestered from rams
And from the bearded goats
With their hairy coats....

John Skelton, "Colin Clout" (1522), 132–59

John Skelton's "Colin Clout," an attack on corrupt, lazy, and stupid clergymen, gives you a fair idea of his style, though he didn't always change rhymes so often. Skelton will happily rhyme twelve lines running if the fancy takes him. Likewise, once he grabs hold of a theme, he's loath to let go, in this case giving up only after 1,270 lines.

Using the well-worn metaphor of shepherds and sheep, Skelton (himself a priest) hammers away at his colleagues for enriching themselves at the expense of their flock. Bishops, in particular, spent lots more time collecting wealth (supposedly for the benefit of the clergy) than delivering sermons. Skelton chalks this up partly to laziness, but mostly to intellectual bankruptcy.

Happily, there are some two or three clerics in England actually devoted to protecting their flocks. These upright shepherds alertly "keep the wolf from the door," to untangle

Skelton's syntax. Though the phrase is used now to mean "stave off poverty," that's not at all what Skelton meant.

First of all, poverty was a virtue in the clergy—he criticizes those determined *not* to be poor. Second of all, while a real shepherd might conceivably starve if a real wolf got to his real sheep, that situation doesn't translate in the metaphor. Skelton's "wolf" is the Devil, and he's after people's souls, which is why Skelton calls the sheep "ghostly" and "spiritual" (the two words are synonyms here). The shepherds are supposed to worry about that wolf, and not about filling their bellies.

Words Are Cheap

Throughout the world, if it were sought,
Fair words enough a man shall find.
They be good cheap; they cost right naught;
Their substance is but only wind.
But well to say and so to mean—
That sweet accord is seldom seen.

Sir Thomas Wyatt, "Throughout
the World" (ca. 1540)

Poets have used their gifts to many ends: to explore emotions, to celebrate nature, to praise God, to philosophize in rhyme, to argue and judge, to seduce and attack. In the Renaissance they used poetry mostly to complain. Sir Thomas Wyatt was king of the whiners.

Some of his verse is merely imitative complaining, which he picked up from the Italian poet Petrarch, who wrote countless elegant love-laments. (By translating and imitating Petrarch's sonnets, Wyatt introduced the form to England.) But the rest is based on his rocky experiences in the hurly-burly court of Henry VIII, one of the most temperamental rulers in human history. Wyatt was constantly slipping in and out of the king's favor, here serving as a highly placed clerk or ambassador, and there serving time in the Tower of London.

This poem is one of his many on the hypocrisy and falsity of the Renaissance political world. It's frankly not the best of them—you'd never guess Wyatt was one of the great English poets before Shakespeare—but it does yield his most enduring coinage: "Words…be good cheap." It costs nothing merely to say something; it still costs nothing to say it eloquently. The trick is to mean it, and in Wyatt's estimation that's a phenomenon "seldom seen."

Besides being the first to have written "Words are cheap," Wyatt also quotes another phrase popular in his day, "Words are but wind." Other gems in this vein included "Words are but words," "From words to deeds is a great space," "Many words will not fill a bushel," "Fair words don't fill the belly," "A man of words and not of deeds is like a garden full of weeds," and so forth. You don't hear this sort of complaint too much anymore, which may only mean that we have lower expectations.

The Merry Month of May

Is not thilke the mery moneth of May,
When love lads masken in fresh aray?
How falles it then, we no merrier bene,
Ylike as others, girt in gawdy greene?
Our bloncket liveryes bene all to sadde,
For thilke same seasone, when all is ycladd
With pleasaunce: the grownd with grasse, the
    Woods
With greene leaves, the bushes with blossoming
    Buds.

Edmund Spenser, *The Shepheardes Calender*
(1579), "May," 1–8

One of the Elizabethans' favorite Classical verse forms was the pastoral allegory, which had reached its peak in Virgil's *Eclogues*. In such poems simple shepherds discourse on country life, which would all be pretty boring except that the whole thing is a disguise for comment on contemporary affairs. Actually, most of it is still boring.

In this specimen of the genre, Edmund Spenser takes up the religious war between Anglicans and Catholics, a major domestic problem in England. Representing the Catholics is Palinode, a priest in the guise of an old Greek shepherd. "Is this not the merry month of May?" he coins to his somber companion, a Protestant minister-cum-shepherd with the distinctly English name Piers. "Is this not the month when sportive young lovers frolic and dance in their new outfits? Then why are we such sticks in the mud, moping about in these dull old gray coats, while all nature is gay and gaily dressed [*yclad with pleasaunce*]?"

This of course is just the sort of thing a debauched, idol-worshipping Catholic would say—a priest no less! Palinode is in for an earful of Piers's stern correction, which drifts from the Protestant to the Puritanical. All these shepherds who indulge in "lustihood and wanton merriment," says Piers, are the Devil's shepherds, not God's. While they're getting their jollies, their neglected sheep roam unfed and unattended.

The minister/shepherd metaphor was stock stuff in Renaissance religious discourse. Spenser wasn't the first to accuse the hated Catholic clergy of abusing its office and leading its flock to the Devil. He seems, however, to have been the first to write "merry month of May." Despite himself, he gave a Catholic the good lines.

Love at First Sight

It lies not in our power to love or hate,
For will in us is overruled by fate.
When two are stripped, long ere the course begin
We wish that one should lose, the other win;
And one especially we do affect
Of two gold ingots, like in each respect.
The reason no man knows, let it suffice,
What we behold is censured by our eyes.
Where both deliberate, the love is slight;
Who ever loved, that loved not at first sight?

Christopher Marlowe, *Hero and Leander*
(ca. 1592), 167–76

With the Classical revival in full swing, Renaissance literature is full of famous couples from the annals of ancient fiction: Pygmalion and Galatea, Pyramus and Thisbe, and the subjects of Christopher Marlowe's witty, racy, unfinished lark, *Hero and Leander*.

Marlowe is better known for his plays, such as *The Jew of Malta* and *Doctor Faustus*—not to mention his shady dealings and violent death in 1593—than for his one narrative poem, but it's a damned good first try. (Shakespeare's first, *Venus and Adonis,* isn't any better.) Written in quick-moving verses and with ironic tone, Marlowe's poem is very much in the style of Ovid, whose earthy mythologies were all the rage.

Hero and Leander was a big hit among London's smart set, and many of its lines became instant quotes. "Who ever loved, that loved not at first sight?" was the biggest winner, nicked with a wink by Shakespeare for *As You Like It*. Shakespeare treats the notion as comic but serious; Marlowe presents it as serious but comic. That is, it looks like a good idea on paper, but Marlowe doesn't really mean it. (Whether he believed anything he wrote is an open question.)

The stanza quoted here is a little philosophical set piece in the middle of our hero, Leander's, first encounter with our heroine, Hero. Leander sees, and loves; Hero, likewise. But this mutual fascination will turn out badly in the end, which prompts the question here as to whether falling in love was the wisest course of action.

The stanza replies that when it comes to love no one has a choice. Whether we like it or not, a powerful outside force—fate—decides whom we love or hate. We can pursue our preferences and judgments in most things (as in favoring one runner in a race, or in choosing between two nearly identical things), but passion overrules judgment (*censure*). In short, conscious decisions have no role in passions: If you *decide* to love someone, it isn't really love.

But being involuntary doesn't require being sudden. You could just as easily fall helplessly in love on fifth or sixth sight, or grow to hate someone irrationally in the course of time. Marlowe joins together two separate ideas—time and fate—in order to fortify both. He's describing a passion so intense, so immediate, and ultimately so fatal, that it betrays the hand of a very determined and very powerful outside force.

A Well-Wrought Urn

We can die by it, if not live by love,
And if unfit for tombs and hearse

∽✕∾

Or legend be, it will be fit for verse;
   And if no piece of chronicle we prove,
     We'll build in sonnets pretty rooms;
     As well a well-wrought urn becomes
The greatest ashes, as half-acre tombs,
     And by these hymns, all shall approve
     Us canonized for love.

             John Donne, "The Canonization"
                   (1590s), 28–36

Any poor soul who's come close to majoring in English will know this line, though not necessarily from Donne. Like "for whom the bell tolls," the "well-wrought urn" gained new life in the twentieth century as a book title, albeit less famously. Critic Cleanth Brooks's *The Well-Wrought Urn* once helped define a whole school of criticism, called "The New Criticism"; but that's all behind us now in the postmodern era.

Luckily, Donne's poem is more durable than any school of lit crit, even if it's had its own ups and downs through the years. "The Canonization," in the humble opinion of this writer, is one of the supreme lyric poems in English. A witty retort to friends who chide him for loving, Donne's poem is also a serious testament to love's power.

In the course of proving love's greatness, Donne admits that it isn't all peaches and cream. There's some pain, of course, and doubts and debilities, but who else is hurt? He then launches into an extended joke on "death," a Renaissance euphemism for orgasm, culminating in the bold claim that if he and his lover aren't exactly living for love, they'll at least be happy to "die by it."

But seriously, sort of, Donne knows that his love isn't the stuff of legends, nor will it be celebrated by his peers in eulogies affixed to his tomb or "hearse" (in those days a wooden structure set over a coffin). But it's good enough for a set of pretty sonnets, which may not be grand like "half-acre tombs," but which, like delicate little "well-wrought urns," equally becomes the ashes of great men, or great loves.

Donne suggests that his poems will so eloquently and lastingly speak of love that readers will canonize him and his girlfriend as love's saints. At this point it's difficult to know to what degree he's kidding.

Death, Be Not Proud

> Death, be not proud, though some have called
> thee
> Mighty and dreadful, for thou art not so;
> For those whom thou think'st thou dost over-
> throw
> Die not, poor Death, nor yet canst thou kill me.

Donne, *Holy Sonnets,* Sonnet 10 (1633), 1–4

Donne was the greatest of the so-called "Metaphysical poets" of the 17th century—and there were many great ones. His *Holy Sonnets* are archetypal Metaphysical poems: philosophical yet immediate and emotional, fond of paradox and contrast, irregular in pacing, simultaneously symbolic and concrete, and concerned with the link of the physical to the spiritual.

Donne's defiant and famous line "Death, be not proud" introduces a Metaphysical riddle: when is death not death? The answer: when death is merely physical.

The poet warns Death—death brought to life as allegory—not to let success go to his head.

Though many have called Death mighty, and though most everyone fears it, Death is really our friend, not our enemy. For one thing, death is just a deeper and more lasting form of sleep, so it can only be more restful and pleasurable. For another thing, the soul is ultimately happy to be free of the body, its prison.

As for Death's supposed power, even that's not very impressive. Death is merely "slave to fate, chance, kings, and desperate men," and it's forced to dwell "with poison, war, and sickness"—not exactly fun company.

And finally, our physical death, intensely restful, is merely a brief prelude before "we wake eternally,/ And death shall be no more." Drawing on the Christian idea of apocalypse, Donne foresees the second coming of Christ, when God shall establish a new eternal kingdom, free of evil, suffering, and death. And then, Donne quips, "Death, thou shalt die."

For Whom the Bell Tolls
and No Man Is an Island

Perchance he for whom this bell tolls may be so
ill as that he knows not it tolls for him; and perchance I may think myself so much better than I
am as that they who are about me and see my
state may have caused it to toll for me, and I
know not that....The bell doth toll for him that
thinks it doth; and though it intermit again, yet
from that minute that the occasion wrought upon

him, he is united to God. Who casts not up his eye to the sun when it rises? but who takes off his eye from a comet when that breaks out? Who bends not his ear to any bell which upon any occasion rings? but who can remove it from that bell which is passing a piece of himself out of this world? No man is an island, entire of itself; every man is a piece of the continent, a part of the main....[A]ny man's death diminishes me because I am involved in mankind, and therefore never send to know for whom the bell tolls; it tolls for thee.

Donne, *Devotions upon Emergent Occasions*
(1624), XVII

A short break from poetry for a taste of Donne's prose, one passage from which yields his two most famous phrases. His *Devotions,* which describe his thoughts as he suffered and survived a grave illness, are moving meditations on human frailty and mortality, composed in a spirit of pious devotion. (Donne had taken holy orders in 1615.)

In this chapter, the book's most powerful, Donne contemplates the sound of the church-bell rung whenever someone is near death. He notes that those for whom it tolls frequently deny the fact, unable to accept that the end is upon them. But why deny, and why despair? The bell signals not a frightful end but a joyous beginning of a new life "united to God."

On the other hand, it's worse to rejoice because the bell tolls for someone else. For even if you're not actually dying, you're still suffering, because "no man is an island." We are all one in God, a single interdependent social/religious organism; so whenever a person dies we lose a piece of ourselves. You needn't inquire for whom the bell tolls; one way or another it tolls for thee.

Note that Donne's original wording was "Never send to know for whom the bell tolls," now misquoted as "Ask not for whom...." There's not a whole lot of difference in meaning, though in Donne's version you have to work a little harder for the answer, which, whether you ask or send for it, turns out to be the same.

Drink to Me Only with Thine Eyes

Drink to me only with thine eyes,
    And I will pledge with mine;
Or leave a kiss but in the cup,
    And I'll not look for wine.
The thirst that from the soul doth rise
    Doth ask a drink divine:
But might I of Jove's nectar sup,
    I would not change for thine.

Ben Jonson, "Song: To Celia" (1616), 1–8

How one's eyes might "drink" isn't something you want to think about too hard. The poet gets the easier part: He only has to "pledge," meaning that if Celia does whatever

Jonson imagines her doing, then he will return his love in a glance.

Why Celia can't just drink with her mouth, and the poet pledge with his, is left unexplained. Perhaps there's some need for discretion, or perhaps Jonson finds something more authentic in the eyes, which, according to the Renaissance cliché, are "windows of the soul." Indeed, the song goes on to praise Celia's soul-restoring powers, comparing her "cup" to Jove's.

The introduction of this pagan deity is a clue that Jonson is drawing on Roman sources. Apparently he'd been dipping into the love letters of the Classical philosopher Flavius Philostratus (second century), who supplies all the poem's conceits. In one passage, Philostratus compares a woman's eyes to drinking cups and fantasizes about sipping from them. In comparison, Jonson's metaphor is tame.

Not of an Age, but For All Time

And though thou hadst small Latin and less Greek,
    From thence to honor thee I would not seek
For names, but call forth thund'ring Aeschylus,
    Euripides, and Sophocles to us,
Pacuvius, Accius, him of Cordova dead,
    To life again, to hear thy buskin tread
And shake a stage; or, when thy socks were on,
    Leave thee alone for the comparison
Of all that insolent Greek or haughty Rome
    Sent forth, or since did from their ashes come.
Triumph, my Britain; thou hast one to show
    To whom all scenes of Europe homage owe.

He was not of an age, but for all time!

Jonson, "To the Memory of My Beloved, The
Author, Mr. William Shakespeare, and What
He Hath Left Us" (1623), 31–43

The publication in 1623 of Shakespeare's First Folio—the original edition of his collected works—was a major literary event. A who's who of contemporary poets gladly hitched their wagons to the book by contributing "commendatory verses," in other words flattering tributes.

Ben Jonson—who could flatter with the best of them—wasn't going to miss this opportunity, though his opinion of Shakespeare was hardly unmixed. In response to the Folio editors' claim that Shakespeare wrote so fluidly and instinctively that he never blotted out a line, Jonson replied, "Would he had blotted a thousand."

A more studied and deliberate writer, Jonson was vain of his craft and of his fidelity to the Classical "rules" of poetry and drama, as propounded for example by the Greek Aristotle and the Roman Horace. Even in his commendation of the "beloved" Shakespeare, he manages to make an invidious comparison to the Bard's deficiencies in Classical learning—his "small Latin and less Greek."

Despite this hint of envy, we can't completely dismiss Jonson's sincerity as he boasts of Shakespeare's achievement, inviting a crew of ancient tragedians to come hear the Bard's "buskin" shake the stage. (The *buskin* or boot was the symbolic footgear of tragedy, as the *sock* was of comedy.) Jonson then confidently proclaims that in both tragedy and comedy Shakespeare has produced works that stand up to the best of any age, and that in fact will shine forever: "He was not of an age, but for all time!"

Jonson was of course correct, even if it stung his pride to say so, and whether or not his praise is entirely heartfelt. (Flattery and exaggeration were the rule in commendatory verse.) The sad part is that Jonson's own plays, which he thought more artful, have suffered in history's esteem partly by comparison to Shakespeare's. True, Jonson's work, full of topical allusions and period satire, is much more "of an age." But if we didn't have *Hamlet* and *King Lear* and *Twelfth Night* and the rest, we might consider *Volpone* and *The Alchemist* the greatest works of English drama.

Gather Ye Rosebuds While Ye May

Gather ye rosebuds while ye may,
    Old time is still a–flying:
And this same flower that smiles today,
    Tomorrow will be dying.

The glorious lamp of heaven, the sun,
    The higher he's a–getting,
The sooner will his race be run,
    And nearer he's to setting.

That age is best which is the first,
    When youth and blood are warmer,
But being spent, the worse, and worst
    Times still succeed the former.

༄

Then be not coy, but use your time,
  And while ye may, go marry:
For having lost but once your prime,
  You may forever tarry.

> Robert Herrick, "To the Virgins, to Make
> Much of Time" (1648)

Many were the Renaissance poems urging young maids to get on with it. Some, like this one, are sprightly and lyrical; others, like Marvell's "To His Coy Mistress" (page 89), are more pressing and blunt. Whatever the tone, the standard argument boils down to this: "You're not getting any younger."

This poem divides into two parts, each of two stanzas. In the first, Herrick appeals to the rhythms of nature and employs the innocent metaphor of picking flowers. Pick them while you can, he says, for the day is getting dark and those flowers are fading. In the second part, he pulls out the heavier guns. You, he tells the virgins, are like those flowers you pick: getting older, but *not* getting better. Once you're past your prime, you can forget about getting "picked" by a husband, and you may be doomed to "forever tarry" in old maidenhood.

All this anxiety about what Shakespeare called "devouring time" ("Sonnet 19") is typical of the age. Read enough Renaissance poetry and you're likely to find much of it depressingly morbid. But this was before the advent of modern medicine, when the average life expectancy was about 35 years. People *had* to worry about gathering their rosebuds, whether or not they were ready.

Stone Walls Do Not a Prison Make

Stone walls do not a prison make,
　　Nor iron bars a cage:
Minds innocent and quiet take
　　That for an hermitage.
If I have freedom in my love,
　　And in my soul am free,
Angels alone, that soar above,
　　Enjoy such liberty.

Richard Lovelace, "To Althea from Prison"
(1648), 25–32

Who Althea was, and whether she ever existed, are questions we can no longer answer. But the prison was certainly real, and Richard Lovelace was in it. A loyal courtier to King Charles I, Lovelace was jailed twice by the anti-royalist Parliament. It was during his second stay that he put together his first collection of poetry, which included "To Althea" (possibly written in his first stint).

The poem proposes that freedom is a state of mind. The body may be confined, but the spirit can still roam free, soaring on wings of truth, loyalty, and love. A physical prison is no prison to him whose spirit is free: "Stone walls do not a prison make."

Lovelace goes farther than this, though; the real power of his poem stems from defiance. Not only does he claim his freedom from within stone walls, he claims that it's a greater freedom *because* he's in prison. This contrast or paradox adds extra lift—his body constrained, his soul flies even higher. This is why he can say that "Angels alone, that soar above, / Enjoy such liberty." I'm sure there have been other condemned men certain of their innocence and love, but it's part and parcel of Lovelace's exaltation that he thinks he alone is in angels' company.

To Play with Fire

> When first my youthful, sinful age
> > Grew master of my ways,
> Appointing error for my Page,
> > And darkness for my days;
> I flung away, and with full cry
> > Of wild affections, rid
> In post for pleasures, bent to try
> > All gamesters that would bid.
> I played with fire, did counsel spurn,
> > Made life my common stake;
> But never thought that fire would burn,
> > Or that a soul could ache.

Henry Vaughan, "The Garland" (1655), 5–16

You probably suspect where this poem is heading, namely toward renouncing youthful folly. But the outcome is actually a bit stranger than that: The speaker does repent, but only after meeting with a "dead man" who commands him to "Desist fond fool, be not undone." One guesses that the poem isn't strictly autobiographical.

Henry Vaughan wrote at a time when the poetic fashion was Baroque—loaded with symbols and full of abrupt turns. The speaker's startling encounter with the ghost is preceded by an extended metaphor featuring youthful folly as the speaker's master, error as his page, wild affections as his posting horse, and danger in the role of fire.

Vaughan not only coined "play with fire," he suggested the follow-up: "and you'll get burned." This is obviously the whole point of the metaphor, just as the usual purpose of depicting youthful folly in poetry is to stamp it out.

The moral, in case you missed it, is summed up in a four-line postscript: Worldly pleasures, like picked flowers, die quickly. If you want something longer-lasting, let the flowers grow (i.e., deny your pleasures), and there will be an eternal garland awaiting you in heaven.

Had We But World Enough and Time

> Had we but world enough and time,
> This coyness, Lady, were no crime.
> We would sit down, and think which way
> To walk, and pass our long love's day....
>   But at my back I always hear
> Time's winged chariot hurrying near,
> And yonder all before us lie
> Deserts of vast eternity.
> Thy beauty shall no more be found,

 ❧

Nor, in thy marble vault, shall sound
My echoing song; then worms shall try
That long-preserv'd virginity,
And your quaint honor turn to dust,
And into ashes all my lust:
The grave's a fine and private place,
But none, I think, do there embrace....

Andrew Marvell, "To His Coy Mistress"
(1681), 1–4, 21–32

If space did not forbid, I'd quote the whole of this exceptional poem, which pulls off the feat of being at once really sleazy and incredibly beautiful.

Its purpose is to seduce, which isn't unusual; nor is the argument that a maid shouldn't cling too long to virginity. What is unusual is the poem's somewhat disgusting frankness, and its bold use of death images as a means of seduction. I guess some people find thoughts of worm-eaten corpses stimulating.

Marvell's basic logic is this: If we had all the time in the world, and a world big enough to play in, I wouldn't mind dallying in eternal foreplay. But we don't have "world enough and time"; time presses at our backs, propelling us toward death, an eternal desert. And if you take your precious virginity to the grave, where you won't hear or feel another thing, then you'll lose it to the worms, who will *try* (violate) your *quaint honor* (both words puns for female genitals).

In short, "let us sport us while we may"—an echo (likely deliberate) of Robert Herrick's "Gather ye rosebuds while ye may" (page 84). Rather than just be slaves to time, let's "devour" it, "And tear our pleasures with rough strife / Through the iron gates of life," meaning:

let's sport us *vigorously.* "Thus," Marvell concludes, "though we cannot make our sun / Stand still, yet we will make him run." It's an exhilarating conclusion, and it certainly has me convinced.

John Milton

John Milton (1608–1674) lived and wrote through one of the great cultural transitions in English history. He was part of the last generation that could conceivably study, if not master, all Western literature, science, and history. Milton pursued this daunting task first at Cambridge and then for five intense years at home. He was also among the last great Humanists, scholars and writers who looked to the Bible for spiritual truths and to the Classics for aesthetic and natural truths.

At the same time, Milton was a man of the future. He was interested in the new science and new philosophy that were gradually supplanting the Classics, and he paid a visit to the imprisoned Galileo while traveling Italy in the late 1630s. More notably, he was a fervent deputy and propagandist at home in the English revolutionary cause. During the 1640s and most of the '50s, he set aside poetry and devoted himself to apologies for the Cromwell regime and grand treatises on government, education, religion, and numerous other contentious topics, often espousing highly advanced and sometimes unpopular views. (He hated any form of censorship, and he labored mightily to prove that the Bible sanctioned divorce.)

During the same period, Milton gradually went blind, thanks partly to his voluminous reading and writing. Things got worse after 1660, when the revolutionaries were tossed out of office and King Charles II returned home from French exile. Milton was briefly imprisoned and most of his property was confiscated, leaving him under virtual house arrest, broken and embittered. His worldly activities thus curtailed, he turned back to poetry and to affairs of the spirit. All his ambitions were for a time channeled into composing a great epic work that would "justify the ways of God to men."

The result, *Paradise Lost,* completed around 1663, was first published in 1667. It was immediately recognized as one of the great works of English literature, and its prestige has never waned. Milton's last poetical works, *Paradise Regained* and *Samson Agonistes,* were published in one volume in 1671. In his last years he also wrote a history of England and various treatises on history, logic, and religion. He died of the gout in 1674.

Trip the Light Fantastic

> Haste thee, Nymph, and bring with thee
> Jest and youthful Jollity,
> Quips and Cranks and wanton Wiles,
> Nods, and Becks, and wreathed Smiles,
> Such as hang on Hebe's cheek,
> And love to live in dimple sleek;
> Sort that wrinkled Care derides,
> And Laughter holding both his sides.
> Come, and trip it as you go
> On the light fantastic toe,
> And in thy right hand lead with thee
> The mountain nymph, sweet Liberty;
> And if I give thee honor due,
> Mirth, admit me of thy crew,
> To live with her, and live with thee,
> In unreproved pleasures free.

"L'Allegro" (ca. 1632), 25–40

If you could still call anything by Milton popular, it would be his pair of portraits, "L'Allegro" ("the light-hearted man") and "Il Penseroso" ("the contemplative man"). Despite the titles, the two gentlemen don't appear to be Italian; in any case, they're more talking allegories than people.

"L'Allegro" and "Il Penseroso" are cousins to old school exercises in arguing both sides of a case—for example, the merits of the active life versus those of the contemplative. L'Allegro is the extroverted, sanguine, active man, and Il Penseroso the introverted, melancholic, contemplative man, and each uses his poem to justify his life. The poetic contest is a draw, though there's no doubt who would win were the case put to a vote.

In the passage quoted here, L'Allegro addresses himself to Mirth, one of the three Graces in Greek mythology. He bids her come sport with him, bringing fun company like Jest and Jollity, Quips and Cranks (witty remarks) and the rest, including Hebe, Jove's jolly cup-bearer.

But he doesn't want her to just slouch in; he wants her to "trip it as ye go / On the light fantastic toe." This obviously makes more sense than the usual quotation, "to trip the light fantastic" (the light fantastic what?), which sounds like stumbling through some peculiar dance. *Trip* means "skip," and Mirth's *light fantastic toe* makes free-spirited, fancifully intricate movements.

In contrast, Il Penseroso says fie to Mirth, and begs another goddess, Melancholy, to be his companion. "Come," he bids her, "but keep thy wonted [usual] state,/ With ev'n step, and musing gait" ("Il Penseroso," 37–38). Il Penseroso manages to toss a similar wet blanket on practically every one of L'Allegro's fancies.

Every Dark Cloud Has a Silver Lining

O welcome pure-ey'd Faith, white-handed Hope,
Thou hov'ring Angel girt with golden wings,
And thou unblemish't form of Chastity,
I see ye visibly, and now believe
That he, the Supreme good, t' whom all things ill
Are but as slavish officers of vengeance,
Would send a glist'ring Guardian, if need were,
To keep my life and honor unassail'd.
Was I deceiv'd, or did a sable cloud
Turn forth her silver lining on the night?
I did not err, there does a sable cloud
Turn forth her silver lining on the night,
And casts a gleam over this tufted Grove.

Comus (1634), 213–25

Milton had a thing for personifications—Jest, Jollity, Quips, Cranks, and so forth in "L'Allegro"; Faith, Hope, and Chastity here. You might wonder if he was given to hallucination; but such beings were a standard part of the poetry kit he knew and loved best. Its instruments, however, are not very subtle.

Comus is a "mask," a short, highly artificial dramatic production, typically staged at a gathering of lords. The only poet ever to write a subtle one was Ben Jonson; Milton takes no chances with subtlety. The plot is as standard as they come: A virtuous radiant damsel (he actually uses the word) is taken captive by an evil magician (Satan's tool), but she bravely defies him and is eventually rescued by her virile and noble young brothers.

The theme is also not surprising: Evil has no power over faith. Lost in a dark forest as night falls, the Damsel is hit with a dose of Comus's magic dust, which fills her mind with all sorts of horrible notions. A "thousand fantasies" of "calling shapes and beck'ning shadows dire" tempt her to despair, but Comus had no idea who he was dealing with. "These thoughts may startle well," pronounces the unfazed Damsel, "but not astound [daze]/ The virtuous mind," ever attended by "a strong sliding champion Conscience" (lines 205–12).

This is when pure-eyed Faith and his crew enter the scene to deliver the message that God ("the Supreme good") has a "glist'ring Guardian" waiting in the wings if required. (*Glister* is an old form of *glitter.*) And as if to prove that He's really there, a black cloud of night turns inside out to reveal a gleaming lining, a moment Milton thought so important he tells us about it twice.

The point, obviously, is that nothing's ever that bad if you believe in God. Seeming evils are merely His "slavish officers," true threats only to the wicked. They are dark clouds, but with a cozy inside. Notice that Milton says *sable,* which more properly means "black" rather than "dark," but somewhere in the course of the phrase's mutation, this half at least became a bit less dramatic.

The Last Infirmity of a Noble Mind

Alas! What boots it with incessant care
To tend the homely slighted Shepherd's trade,
And strictly meditate the thankless Muse?
Were it not better done as others use,

To sport with Amaryllis in the shade,
Or with the tangles of Neaera's hair?
Fame is the spur that the clear spirit doth raise
(That last infirmity of Noble mind)
To scorn delights, and live laborious days;
But the fair Guerdon when we hope to find,
And think to burst out into sudden blaze,
Comes the blind Fury with th'abhorred shears,
And slits the thin-spun life.

"Lycidas" (1637), 64–76

We stray from Milton's coinage when we say "Ambition is the last infirmity of the noble mind." But our meaning remains true to the original: Great minds find it hardest to overcome the desire for fame. Which isn't so bad as vices go. As Milton says, it encourages "clear spirits" (virtuous minds) to work hard. (Lazy virtue, or unrealized virtue, isn't really virtue at all.)

But what good is pursuit of fame—which is laborious, after all—if we never reap the fruit? What if, as we labor toward the "fair Guerdon" (fine reward), our lives are cut short? Everything becomes nothing as the "blind Fury," Atropos (one of the three Greek Fates), takes out her big scissors and snips the thread of life. (This *Fate* is a counterpart to *Fame,* also a Classical goddess.)

The reason Milton asks is that an old college friend and fellow poet, Edward King, has recently drowned on the Irish Sea. King is the Lycidas of the poem's title, and the poem is a Classical pastoral elegy, verse in praise of the dead, written in the voice of a simple shepherd-poet.

So when Milton refers to the "shepherd's trade," he's referring to poetry, a.k.a. "strictly meditating the thankless Muse" (working hard at verse with no reward). That last line

Milton borrowed from Virgil, and the more famous "infirmity" line is based on another Classical writer, Tacitus. In Book IV of his *Histories,* Tacitus says that "Love of glory is the last thing even wise men can bear to be parted from."

But what is the answer to the poet's question? Why indeed work hard, perhaps for nothing, when we could be enjoying ourselves in dalliance with pretty nymphs like Amaryllis and Neaera? Because true Fame is not really celebrity or popularity; true Fame is recognition in Heaven. And God keeps track of how hard we work.

Look Homeward Angel

> Ay me! Whilst thee the shores and sounding Seas
> Wash far away, where'er thy bones are hurl'd,
> Whether beyond the stormy Hebrides,
> Where thou perhaps under the whelming tide
> Visit'st the bottom of the monstrous world;
> Or whether thou to our moist vows denied,
> Sleep'st by the fable of Bellerus old,
> Where the great vision of the guarded Mount
> Looks toward Namancos and Bayona's hold;
> Look homeward Angel now, and melt with ruth:
> And, O ye Dolphins, waft the hapless youth.

"Lycidas" (1637), 154–64

Here's another verse better known as the title of someone else's book (see also "Remembrance of Things Past," page 53; "For Whom the Bell Tolls," page 79; and "Far from the Madding Crowd," page 130). The borrower this time was the American Thomas Wolfe, for a semi-autobiographical novel published in 1929; his original touch was to add a comma after "Homeward."

The "Angel" in question is St. Michael the Archangel, one of God's most powerful and trusted agents. Milton finds him standing guard atop St. Michael's Mount in Cornwall, "by the fable of Bellerus old," a mythical character who the Romans thought roamed the Cornish coast.

But let's untangle this convoluted sentence from the start. As noted in the previous entry, "Lycidas" is an elegy for Milton's friend Edward King, who drowned in the Irish Sea and whose body was never recovered. Thus no one knows where the "sounding Seas" have washed his bones—they could be anywhere from the sea's extreme north (the Scottish Hebrides) to its extreme south (Land's End in Cornwall), both places home to ancient monsters.

As the poet sweeps from north to south, arriving at Cornwall, he finds the figure of St. Michael, more comforting and more powerful than any pagan fable. The saint's usual duty is to keep an eye on "Namancos" and "Bayona," old launching pads, in northwestern Spain, for the dread Spanish Armada. But the poet asks him to turn his protective gaze away for a moment from enemy territory, toward home, to "melt with ruth." (*Ruth* is an old word for "pity"; thus *ruthless* means "pitiless.")

While he's at it, Milton also attempts to enlist a few dolphins in recovering the bones. Dolphins were known, in old myths, to rescue bodies from the seas. Though we can't blame the poet for turning everywhere for help, the jumping back and forth from pagan to Christian figures is a little disconcerting. Elsewhere Milton condemns all Classical myth as erroneous if not Satanic, but here the mythic dolphins get to trump an archangel, who just stands there full of pity.

To Justify the Ways of God to Men

> And chiefly thou, O Spirit, that dost prefer
> Before all temples th' upright heart and pure,
> Instruct me, for thou know'st; thou from the first
> Wast present, and, with mighty wings outspread,
> Dovelike sat'st brooding on the vast abyss,
> And mad'st it pregnant: what in me is dark
> Illumine; what is low, raise and support;
> That to the height of this great argument
> I may assert Eternal Providence,
> And justify the ways of God to men.
>
> *Paradise Lost* (1667), Book I, 17–26

In writing the one great English epic, and one of the two great Christian epics (along with Dante's *Divine Comedy*), Milton built on the foundation of the pagan classics, chief among them Homer's *Iliad* and Virgil's *Aeneid*. What to do with undeniably powerful but undeniably heathen traditions is always a live issue in Milton's poetry, and it's never comfortably resolved. In general, though, he co-opts them in order to transcend them, as in the introduction to *Paradise Lost,* where the traditional epic invocation of the Muse becomes an invocation of a greater inspirer, the Holy Spirit of the Christian Trinity.

Milton modestly appeals to the Spirit for help in achieving "Things unattempted yet in prose or rhyme" (line 16)—namely, to flesh out and rationalize the Bible's account of Adam and Eve. Milton, who knew the entire Bible by heart, knew that the early books of Genesis are a little hard to swallow, examined rationally, and that they are silent on major points of Christian doctrine (for example, the rebellion of Satan and the creation of Hell).

While he doesn't change the Biblical story, Milton adds a great deal, including various philosophical debates, several major characters, and a big epic showdown between the forces of Good and Evil. All this extra material, which makes the Genesis story at once more plausible, more exciting, and more Christian, is directed at a single purpose: to "justify the ways of God to men" (line 26).

Perhaps you're wondering why God needs justifying, as if He couldn't take care of Himself. This is the eternal paradox of human preaching: God uses, and requires, men to explain His ways to other men. As human inquiry and discovery continue to expand, old explanations and beliefs become inadequate, requiring new interpretations and new additions to the original story.

Milton succeeded spectacularly. Even though, as a fervent adherent of Cromwell and the Puritan cause, he was a social and political outcast in the early Restoration, Milton's epic justification was universally celebrated. His por-

trayal of the war of the angels—Satan's versus God's—and
of the temptation and fall of man took a quick and lasting
hold in the English mind.

For example, he singlehandedly re-created Satan as a
great tragic figure, where before the devil was portrayed
as a two-dimensional monster or clown. Milton also
firmly established that the forbidden fruit was an apple,
though the author of Genesis probably had in mind a
pomegranate or date.

These literary additions to the Hebrew tale continued, and continue, to exert their power—the tragic Satan,
for instance, would play a large role in Romantic poetry.
On the other hand, Milton's logic—which is to say his
justification—has had its ups and downs. What he claims
to justify is the Fall of Man itself: how it happened, and
why God let it happen, even though it meant suffering,
discord, and death for mankind. As we shall see, Milton
had his work cut out for him on this score; his answer,
built on logical and legal reasoning, seems rather uncon-
vincing today. Many critics have questioned whether Milton believed it himself. William Blake, noting that the
tragic Satan is much more appealing than Milton's legalis-
tic God, went so far as to claim that as "a true Poet," Milton was "of the Devil's party without knowing it."

Darkness Visible

> At once as far as Angels' ken he views
> The dismal Situation waste and wild,
> A Dungeon horrible, on all sides round

As one great Furnace flam'd, yet from those
    flames
No light, but rather darkness visible
Serv'd only to discover sights of woe,
Regions of sorrow, doleful shades, where peace
And rest can never dwell, hope never comes
That comes to all; but torture without end
Still urges, and a fiery Deluge, fed
With ever-burning Sulphur unconsum'd:
Such place Eternal Justice had prepar'd
For those rebellious, here their Prison ordained
In utter darkness....

Paradise Lost, Book I, 59–72

After a lengthy invocation, Milton begins his story with Satan, its villain, on his back in a lake of fire, taking a first look around his new home in Hell. This wasteland of darkness and despair is his reward for raising "impious War" against "the Throne and Monarchy of God" (lines 41–42). It is the first of the poem's many little ironies that Milton himself, blind and impoverished, wrote *Paradise Lost* from a private hell, where he was cast when his party lost its war against the "Throne and Monarchy" of England.

Whatever you make of that fact, it's doubtless that Milton's blindness resonates in his descriptions of "darkness," a word that figures twice in this passage. The more striking instance is "darkness visible," an uncanny paradox whose mystery symbolizes God's terrible power to fashion the impossible. Though we cannot envision such a thing as visible darkness, we can feel its meaning.

Milton's entire picture of Hell is built on dreamlike and sometimes contradictory images—the hope that comes to "all," but not to the angels in Hell; the sulfur that burns eternally without being consumed (that is, without burning). To use more modern symbolism, Hell is the antimatter to Heaven's matter, a place of pure negation and endless torture.

You can also read "darkness visible" psychologically, as a symbol of the black awareness of the tortured soul. (This reading inspired William Styron to title his memoir on depression *Darkness Visible*.) The darkness may not be a literal property of the hellfire surrounding him, but more a property of Satan's mind.

Satan himself eventually comes around to the psychological view of things. As he speeds his way to Earth to make mischief in the Garden of Eden, he doesn't leave Hell behind—rather, "within him Hell / He brings" (Book IV, lines 20–21). "Me miserable!" Satan cries;

> which way shall I fly
> Infinite wrath and infinite despair?
> Which way I fly is Hell; myself am Hell....

> (IV, 73–75)

Better to Reign in Hell, Than Serve in Heaven

> Farewell happy Fields
> Where Joy for ever dwells: Hail horrors, hail
> Infernal world, and thou profoundest Hell
> Receive thy new Possessor: One who brings
> A mind not to be chang'd by Place or Time.
> The mind is its own place, and in itself

Can make a Heav'n of Hell, a Hell of Heav'n.
What matter where, if I be still the same,
And what I should be, all but less than he
Whom Thunder hath made greater? Here at least
We shall be free; th' Almighty hath not built
Here for his envy, will not drive us hence:
Here we may reign secure, and in my choice
To reign is worth ambition though in Hell:
Better to reign in Hell, than serve in Heav'n.

Paradise Lost, Book I, 249–63

For *Paradise Lost* Milton adopted a poetic form, blank verse, which till then had mainly been reserved for drama. And the verse suits nothing in his poem so well as the dramatic, tragic monologues of the antihero Satan, who's appealing to the degree he's histrionic. He knows how to give a crowd-pleasing speech, and this is one of them.

This speech will turn out to be more inspiring to his dispirited comrades in evil—who have just been cast into the darkness visible of Hell—than convincing to himself. For the moment, though, he speaks as if he truly believes that it's "Better to reign in Hell, than serve in Heav'n," as if he really had a choice.

In fact, it's a delusion, just like the rest of his speech. True, he freely chose to rebel against God; but his equation of obedience with servitude is a false equation, because faithfulness to God involved no sacrifice and extracted no cost. All in all, it was as cushy an existence as an angel could hope for. It was sheer vanity—and rage at the fact that he, like all creatures, is subordinate to God's power—that prompted Satan's rebellion.

Also false is the notion that he's going to "reign in Hell." He thinks he's the "Possessor" of the demons' new home, but in reality he's a prisoner; God built the jail, and He could destroy it in an instant if He wanted to. As if responding to such an objection, Satan then says (line 255) that the physical place doesn't matter, and that Heaven and Hell are mere states of mind that the individual has power to change.

There's some truth to that idea, psychologically speaking (see the previous entry), but in Milton's day denying the physical reality of Heaven *or* Hell was heresy. Even granting the symbolic qualities of Hell's "darkness visible," Satan and his minions are really still in Hell, and it's certainly never going to look or feel like Heaven.

Another of Satan's many mistakes is to think that he and God are of the same class. He even goes so far as to claim that he's the practical equal of God, save that God ("he / Whom Thunder hath made greater") is better armed. Yet all of Satan's subsequent attempts to get even with God backfire in a major way. Even his supposed triumph—leading mankind into sin—plays into a much larger divine plan, ultimately leading only to Satan's total humiliation and final punishment.

Satan's boast about reigning in Hell is a parody of a famous saying by Julius Caesar. According to the historian Plutarch, who wrote biographies of antiquity's great men, Caesar once said that he'd "rather be the chiefest man" in an impoverished Alpine village "than the second person in Rome" (*The Life of Julius Caesar*). Other Satans in prior poems had said similar things; Milton's is the definitive English version.

Pandemonium

> Meanwhile the winged Heralds by command
> Of Sovran power, with awful Ceremony
> And Trumpets' sound throughout the Host pro-
>   claim
> A solemn Council forthwith to be held
> At Pandæmonium, the high Capitol
> Of Satan and his Peers....

> *Paradise Lost,* Book I, 752–57

Milton added lots of great poetry to the English canon, but few new words to the English language. *Pandemonium* is the important exception. (Another poet, Henry More, had already coined *Pandæmoniothen* in 1642, but he was ignored.)

Though Satan and his crew of fallen angels can really cause a commotion, that's not what Milton's "Pandæmonium" means. Its literal sense is "place of all demons," from *pan-* ("all" in Greek) plus *daimon* ("spirit"), with the Latin noun-maker *-ium* tacked on. Though *pandemonium* (which lost its *æ* diphthong in the 19th century) would come to refer to Hell generally, in Milton's original it is the Capitol of Hell, a place where "all demons" gather for important political events.

Gradually, after having been used to mean "Hell" or "wicked place" for a few centuries, the word came to describe its imagined state: chaos, confusion, noise, and uproar. (In Milton the gathering is fairly orderly, but no matter.) The first use of *pandemonium* in this sense is found in historian Francis Parkman's *Pioneers of France in the New World* (1865): "When night came, it brought with

it a pandemonium of dancing and whooping, drumming and feasting." Those Frenchmen.

You may have noticed that the Greek *daimon* is translated above as "spirit." In Homer, the word refers to a god's activity or power; later Greeks personified this power, and *daimon* then meant a quasidivine spirit who carried out a god's orders on Earth. Still later it was said that each person has his or her own *daimon,* a small personal god or guardian.

The early Christians who brought their faith to the Greek world had to find something to do with these *daimones,* because the people insisted on believing in them. Their tactic was to convince their pagan converts that the Greek pantheon was really a pandemonium: full of evil spirits rather than benevolent gods.

In English, *demon* was originally used in both its positive and negative senses—guardian angel and nasty devil. Milton, who seems to have decided that the old gods of Greece and Rome were really lesser devils in Satan's service, naturally adopted the negative sense in coining *pandemonium*.

To Fall on Evil Days

Half yet remains unsung, but narrower bound
Within the visible Diurnal Sphere;
Standing on Earth, not rapt above the Pole,
More safe I Sing with mortal voice, unchang'd
To hoarse or mute, though fall'n on evil days,
On evil days though fall'n, and evil tongues;
In darkness, and with dangers compast round,
And solitude; yet not alone, while thou
Visit'st my slumbers Nightly, or when Morn
Purples the East: still govern thou my Song,
Urania, and fit audience find, though few.

Paradise Lost, Book VII, 21–31

The first half of Milton's epic is mainly a history of Heaven and Hell. As he descends from these lofty heights to train his focus on Earth, Milton heaves a sigh of relief—"More safe I Sing with mortal voice." He's glad to have his feet back on the ground.

But in landing on the ground Milton is also reminded of his painful mortal circumstances. He has, in his words, "fall'n on evil days." Lingering momentarily on this note, he repeats the line in reverse, a favorite Miltonic device for adding special weight and significance to a line.

This is practically the sole exception to Milton's avoidance of self-pity in *Paradise Lost*. As you may recall (page 101), he was writing in a state of "darkness," being blind, and "with dangers compast round," being viewed as an enemy of the state. Milton had been a propagandist and government official during the interregnum, when Cromwell ruled. Once the monarchists returned to power in 1660, he was briefly imprisoned and then fined into poverty.

Even after he was free, he feared for his life. Danger and his contemplative temperament led him to spend his solitary days reading and composing. His only comfort was the visitation of his Muse (Urania), in dreams or as he awoke; and his only hope that his great work would "a fit audience find, though few."

Eyeless in Gaza

Why was my breeding order'd and prescrib'd
As of a person separate to God,
Design'd for great exploits; if I must die
Betray'd, Captiv'd, and both my Eyes put out,
Made of my Enemies the scorn and gaze;
To grind in Brazen Fetters under task
With this Heav'n-gifted strength? O glorious strength
Put to the labor of a Beast, debas't
Lower than bondslave! Promise was that I
Should Israel from Philistian yoke deliver;
Ask for this great Deliverer now, and find him
Eyeless in Gaza at the Mill with slaves,
Himself in bonds under Philistian yoke....

Samson Agonistes (1671), 30–42

Milton based his last poem, a closet tragedy, on the Biblical story of Samson and Delilah. The story begins as the children of Israel do evil yet again in the sight of the Lord, which results in forty years of subjection to their enemies the Philistines.

But the Lord also plans their salvation. He sends an angel to the wife of a certain Manoah to promise that she shall "conceive, and bear a son; and no razor shall come on his head: for the child shall be a Nazarite unto God from the womb: and he shall begin to deliver Israel out of the hand of the Philistines" (Judges 13:5, King James Version).

That savior, Samson, echoes the angel in Milton's poem: "Promise was that I / Should Israel from Philistian yoke deliver." Except that things aren't going too well. His first mistake was to become the lover of Delilah, a Philistine woman; his second mistake was to tell her about his hair. Samson belonged to a reclusive Israelite cult, the Nazarites, which forbade members from cutting their hair. In Samson's case the taboo is especially strong; as he says to Delilah in Judges, "if I be shaven, then my strength will go from me, and I shall become weak, and be like any other man" (16:17).

The rest of the story, in brief, is that Delilah arranges for a shave, Samson is captured and blinded, and the Philistines bring him to Gaza to grind grain in a prison. It is this precipitous fall from glory to humiliation, promise to suffering, that Milton captures in the phrase "eyeless in Gaza." The humiliation is emphasized in *Gaza*'s echo of the gloating Philistines' *gaze* (line 34), which they train on Samson, but which he can't return.

As noted above (page 109), Milton pretty well checked his bitterness and self-pity in *Paradise Lost*; but in Samson's complaining and moaning he finally lets loose.

He too was blind, and he too a virtual prisoner in the Gaza of Restoration England. This equation makes the royalist party into Philistines—a nice little cut, except that in 1671 the word *philistine* did not yet mean "tasteless boor." That meaning would arise a little later in Germany, making it to England only in the 18th century.

Samson eventually did fulfill the Biblical prophecy, by pulling down the pillars of a great hall full of Philistine VIPs. Of course he gets crushed along with them, which doesn't exactly leave Milton with promising options, if he really identified with Samson.

Alexander Pope

Alexander Pope (1688–1744) was the first English poet to earn a living selling books—a feat not often repeated since. His big best-seller was a very fine translation of Homer's *Iliad,* but he earned his place in literary history by his original works, most notably *An Essay on Criticism* (1711) and *The Rape of the Lock* (1712–1714).

Pope's unprecedented success came despite formidable handicaps, including constant physical pain resulting from a childhood disease. He was also born to Catholic parents at a time of fierce popular hostility to "papists"—the year of his birth saw the "Glorious Revolution," when Catholic King James II was driven from the throne into French exile. For this and other reasons he had no formal education but acquired an astonishing body of knowledge by himself—at age 15, he could read Greek, Latin, French, and Italian.

Like many unwilling outsiders (such as Ben Jonson, Catholic son of a bricklayer), Pope excelled at satire. A natural disposition toward social critique and literary polemic was strengthened by association with a group of London wits, including Jonathan Swift and the poet John Gay. Pope found the perfect vehicle for his satire in the "heroic couplet," a rhymed couplet in iambic pentameter, which he employed in every major work.

Pope achieved fame in his day not only as a writer but also, curiously enough, as a gardener. Precluded by his infirmity, his religion, and his temperament from any more ambitious labor, he fell in love with his Twickenham

A Little Learning Is a Dangerous Thing

A little Learning is a dang'rous Thing;
Drink deep, or taste not the Pierian Spring:
There shallow Draughts intoxicate the Brain,
And drinking largely sobers us again.

An Essay on Criticism, Part 2, 215–18

If you're wondering why Pope's *Essay on Criticism* is called an essay when it's really a poem, it's because in the original sense an *essay* could be any informal attempt (*essai* in French) to capture the spirit of a subject; prose was not required.

In this instance Pope draws on two other verse essays in literary criticism, Horace's *Ars Poetica* and the Horatian *L'Art Poétique* by French poet-critic Nicolas Boileau, a generation older than Pope. Like its predecessors, *An Essay on*

Criticism is learned and yet straightforward, though in places it's rather more caustic.

The poem attacks bad criticism as much as it defines the good, and among the failings Pope condemns is "Pride, the never-failing Vice of Fools" (line 204). Its cause is knowing just enough to think oneself learned, but not enough to recognize one's ignorance. The same goes for poets as for critics: A small taste of art leads to arrogance and overconfidence in one's talents.

In short, "A little Learning is a dang'rous Thing." If you intend either to write poetry or to criticize poets, you can't just sip at the "Pierian spring," famed fountain of the Greek Muses. The poetic dilettante giddily attempts to scale the "Heights of Arts," but only makes a fool of himself in the process. More learning teaches us the difficulty of that goal.

To Err Is Human; to Forgive, Divine

> To what base Ends, and by what abject Ways,
> Are Mortals urg'd thro' Sacred Lust of Praise!
> Ah ne'er so dire a Thirst of Glory boast,
> Nor in the Critick let the Man be lost!
> Good-Nature and Good-Sense must ever join;
> To Err is Humane; to Forgive, Divine.

An Essay on Criticism, Part 2, 520–25

Pope was not a man to suffer fools gladly. Witness *The Dunciad,* an attack on his critics he wrote not once, but twice (first in 1728 and anew in 1743). Even in the relatively mild *Essay on Criticism,* which Pope wrote at age 21, the dismissals of "fools" and "blockheads" are unrelenting.

Nonetheless, Pope advises the critic to go easy on poetic folly, no matter how tempting the target. "Avoid Extreams," he counsels (line 384); "and shun the Fault of such, / Who still [always] are pleas'd too little, or too much." It shows little sense to get worked up over trifling things such as bad poems. Furthermore, harsh criticism smacks of self-inflation, as if by attacking the poet one proves oneself superior.

"To Err is Humane," Pope memorably writes; "to Forgive, Divine." By *humane* Pope means "human" (the two meanings once shared a spelling), but he's also talking about being *humane* in our sense. "Nor in the Critick let the Man be lost" means "don't let your critical zeal cloud over your fellow-feeling." Be gentle with the mediocre; save your harshness for more important things.

Pope thought up the part about forgiveness, but the first half of his epigram was a familiar saying. "To err is human" traces back to the Latin proverb *Humanum est errare,* first found first in Seneca's *Naturales Quæstiones* (1st century A.D.). It was quoted and translated numerous times in earlier English literature.

Pope's less banal version may owe something to St. Augustine, who in a sermon said that "It is human to err, diabolical to spitefully remain in error," thus introducing the religious element. Augustine himself may have borrowed the parallelism from Cicero, who said in the *Philippics* that "All men err; but only the fool perseveres in error," which brings us right back to fools.

Fools Rush in Where Angels Fear to Tread

> The Bookful Blockhead, ignorantly read,
> With Loads of Learned Lumber in his Head,
> With his own Tongue still edifies his Ears,
> And always List'ning to Himself appears....
> No Place so Sacred from such Fops is barr'd,
> Nor is Paul's Church more safe than Paul's
>   Church-yard:
> Nay, fly to Altars; there they'll talk you dead;
> For Fools rush in where Angels fear to tread.

An Essay on Criticism,
Book 3, 610–13, 622–25

Pope asks us to forgive human error, then resumes his attacks on human folly. His targets here are bookish but witless critics who not only find fault with everything, they also never shut up.

There is no refuge from these "blockheads," not even a church; they'll follow you right up to the altar, a place where "Angels fear to tread." Pope's particular example is St. Paul's in London, which in his day as in Shakespeare's was as much a place of chit-chat as a place of worship. (The equally fool-flocked churchyard was an old booksellers' haunt.)

Today the quip rarely pertains to literary critics. Like many of Pope's zingers, it arose from a particular situation but is so universally true that it almost begs to be quoted out of context—it's a portable witticism. Examples of the genre abound in his works, and fools are often their victim. At times Pope's wit is less than humane, but as he explains in the "Epistle to Dr. Arbuthnot," "You think me cruel? take it for a rule, / No creature smarts so little as a fool."

Hope Springs Eternal

Hope humbly then; with trembling pinions soar;
Wait the great teacher Death, and God adore!
What future bliss, he gives not thee to know,
But gives that Hope to be thy blessing now.
Hope springs eternal in the human breast:
    Man never Is, but always To be blest:
The soul, uneasy and confin'd from home,
Rests and expatiates in a life to come.

An Essay on Man, Epistle I (1733), 91–98

Having amused himself, and perturbed the literati, with a series of satires including the mock-epic *Dunciad,* Pope was eager to make a more serious, more philosophical contribution to his age. First published anonymously (so as to disarm his critics), *An Essay on Man* begins seriously indeed, with an epistle on "the Nature and State of Man with respect to the Universe."

It cannot be said that Pope decisively settled the issue, but he did contribute a few enduring lines on human nature, this being the most famous: "Hope springs eternal in the human breast." What makes this line great is that its meaning is instantly clear, even out of context. Pope captures the joy and freshness of hope (with the verb *springs*), while also implying that it's rarely borne out: that hope's *eternal* springing is a persistent and irrational response to an eternally disappointing present.

Pope's phrase is popular also because it works in all sorts of situations, whenever optimism persists despite the evidence. But Pope was talking about a particular sort of hope: the hope of those uncertain of their place in the universe, present and future.

Pope is responding to what we might now call "existential anxiety." So, his argument goes, life is hard and painful and often seemingly pointless. But God probably had a good reason for putting Man in this spot, short of perfection; and it's probably best that we don't understand the reason, which might just drive us mad. Besides, God has also prepared a much better life for us after death. We are not given to see or understand this "future bliss," but we know it's there because God has planted hope in the human heart.

Obviously, such hope doesn't spring eternal in every single breast—suicides don't usually act to speed the arrival of bliss. But Pope was speaking of aggregate humanity, the collective human breast.

The Proper Study of Mankind

Know then thyself, presume not God to scan;
The proper study of Mankind is Man.
Plac'd on this isthmus of a middle state,
A being darkly wise, and rudely great:
With too much knowledge for the Sceptic side,
With too much weakness for the Stoic's pride,
He hangs between; in doubt to act, or rest,
In doubt to deem himself a God, or Beast....

An Essay on Man, Epistle II (1733), 1–8

Pope has just rousingly summed up the first epistle (page 117) by declaring Man blissfully ignorant of God's design, which, because it's God's, is good. The last words— "Whatever IS, IS RIGHT"—pretty well sums up Pope's view of the Universe.

In the second epistle, he turns back to the world as it is to consider Man's individuality. Since it's not our business to study God's reasons, we must find something else to do; and the appropriate thing to do is study what's in our compass, namely ourselves.

For authority, Pope reaches back to the dawn of Western philosophy. "Know thyself" is an old Greek epigram attributed to Thales of Miletus, who invented philosophy as he said

it. And though his phrasing is original, Pope hardly invented the idea that "The proper study of Mankind is Man." Besides being a direct translation from *Of Wisdom,* by the 16th-century French philosopher Pierre Charron, it paraphrases another old Greek saying, "Man is the measure of all things."

The idea, preached by the Sophist philosopher Protagoras, is that we know things only in their relation to ourselves. Pope would agree—that's partly why our knowledge is limited. It's also why in order to understand anything we must first understand the measuring device. Man's particular nature, Pope then says, is to be stuck in a middle between God and the beasts—wise, but not very wise; great, but not very great.

So though some Greeks had the right idea, others were wrong. Pope singles out the Skeptics, who underestimated reason's power, and the Stoics, who underestimated emotion's power. We're both emotional and rational, bestial and Godlike. Not a particularly stunning or novel observation, but that's why Pope is better remembered as a poet than as a philosopher.

To Damn with Faint Praise

Were there One whose fires
True Genius kindles, and fair Fame inspires,
Blest with each Talent and each Art to please,
And born to write, converse, and live with ease:
Shou'd such a man, too fond to rule alone,
Bear, like the Turk, no brother near the throne,
View him with scornful, yet with jealous eyes,
And hate for Arts that caus'd himself to rise;

Damn with faint praise, assent with civil leer,
And without sneering, teach the rest to sneer;
Willing to wound, and yet afraid to strike,
Just hint a fault, and hesitate dislike;...
Who but must laugh, if such a man there be?
Who would not weep, if Atticus were he?

"An Epistle from Mr. Pope to
Dr. Arbuthnot" (1735), 192–204, 214–15

Besides his funny name, Dr. John Arbuthnot, physician to
Queen Anne, can lay two claims to fame: inventing John
Bull, the prototypical Englishman, and receiving a very
public poetic epistle from his friend Pope.

Actually, Pope might have sent this "letter" to any of
his pals, since nothing in it pertains particularly to
Arbuthnot. In fact, its real intended audience was a
coterie of spiteful enemies, most of whom have faded to
obscurity. An exception is the target of this passage, the
famous essayist Joseph Addison.

Addison, who had been dead 16 years by the time
the "Epistle" was published, was a great Classical scholar
and essayist, as well as a Member of Parliament. The dean
of a London literary circle, Addison was also jealous of his
prominence and influence. Though Addison had praised
the *Essay on Criticism* as a "Master-piece," he changed his
tune once Pope, who remained aloof from Addison's circle, began achieving real success.

In particular, when he heard in 1715 that Pope was
working on translating the *Iliad,* Addison prompted a
protégé named Thomas Tickell to rush out a competing
translation. This envious tactic failed, but nonetheless
Pope took offense, penning some satirical lines in
response. This passage from the "Epistle"—in which

Addison appears as "Atticus," a Roman literary man—is a revised version.

Pope's essential complaint is that Addison is both too *fond* (vain) to share his literary limelight, and too cowardly to directly *strike* his rivals. When not teaching others to sneer, he writes grudging reviews whose hostility is masked in seeming civility. To quote one of Pope's most famous lines, Addison "Damns with faint praise"—that is, condemns what he despises by praising it in a patently insincere fashion.

In the end Pope finds all this rather sad, since Addison was a man of "True Genius" and "Talent." Time did heal some of the wounds, and on Addison's death in 1719 Pope wrote a moving tribute. But the wounds weren't sufficiently healed to keep Pope from reviving his complaint in the "Epistle."

To Break a Butterfly on a Wheel

A Lash like mine no honest man shall dread,
But all such babling blockheads in his stead.
    Let Sporus tremble—"What? that Thing of silk,
"Sporus, that mere white Curd of Ass's milk?
"Satire or Sense alas! can Sporus feel?
"Who breaks a Butterfly upon a Wheel?"
Yet let me flap this Bug with gilded wings,
This painted Child of Dirt that stinks and stings;
Whose Buzz the Witty and the Fair annoys,
Yet Wit ne'er tastes, and Beauty ne'er enjoys,
So well-bred Spaniels civilly delight
In mumbling of the Game they dare not bite.

"Epistle to Dr. Arbuthnot," 303–14

Having dispatched his one serious enemy—Joseph Addison (page 121)—Pope turns to lesser irritants. His victim in this passage, in the guise of "Sporus," is Lord John Hervey, effeminate author of a few malicious pamphlets against Pope. (Sporus was a Roman courtier castrated and humiliated by Nero.)

Pope adduces Hervey/Sporus as an example of the kind of conceited, foppish "blockhead" who attacks perfectly healthy satire because he spies himself in the satirist's mirror. But even as Pope prepares to demolish this fool, the voice of friend breaks in. What—the friend cries—is the sense of training your heavy satiric weaponry on so trivial a target, a "mere white Curd of Ass's milk"?

That's a cutting line, but even better is the next: "Who breaks a Butterfly upon a Wheel?" The *wheel* in question is an old instrument of torture; supposed offenders were strapped to a large wheel and then their bones were broken. (The phrase "break on a torture," alluding to the same device, traces to 1598; "break upon a wheel" to 1634.) Thus "to break a butterfly [up]on a wheel" is to marshal excessive force against an insignificant threat. More recent versions of the same idea include "to squash a fly with a sledgehammer" and "to douse a match with a fire hose."

Pope doesn't bother to argue with his friend, but just merrily proceeds to pin Hervey to the wheel. In the small excerpt quoted here, he condemns the lord as a small, filthy "bug" merely painted with honor, jabbing at those whose virtues he lacks. He then compares Hervey to a pampered dog that growls when he dares not bite. This goes on for several dozen more lines.

A Ruling Passion

> Judge we by Nature? Habit can efface,
> Int'rest o'ercome, or Policy take place:
> By Actions? those Uncertainty divides:
> By Passions? these Dissimulation hides:
> Opinions? they still take a wider range:
> Find, if you can, in what you cannot change.
>   Search then the Ruling Passion: There, alone,
> The Wild are constant, and the Cunning known;
> The Fool consistent, and the False sincere;
> Priests, Princes, Women, no dissemblers here.

Epistles to Several Persons,
"Epistle I" (1734), 168–77

In his collected *Works* of 1735, Pope compiled four moral essays in verse under the rubric *Epistles to Several Persons.* Like the "Epistle to Dr. Arbuthnot," they're letters only nominally, being dedicated to their recipient but intended for the general public.

The first of these—actually written third—is a treatise on "the Knowledge and Characters of Men," that is, on how to truly judge a person's character. Pope considers numerous possible guides, including one's *nature* (basic temperament), *actions, passions* (feelings), and *opinions,* all of which he discards. Nature is unstable, since it can be overcome by habits or expedient policies; actions stem from a variety of motivations, which are often inconsistent; true feelings are often hidden from an observer; and opinions are also variable, inconsistent, and deceptive.

Which leaves, according to Pope, a person's "Ruling Passion"—not an ordinary feeling, but a central driving motive, which cannot be hidden because it overcomes willy-nilly all other forces, intellectual, emotional, political, or social. "The ruling Passion," says Pope in a later epistle, "be it what it will, / The ruling Passion conquers reason still" ("Epistle III," 155–56).

Simply because it is so relentless, consistent, and uncontrollable, the ruling passion is our only sure guide to a person's character. For an example Pope points to Philip, Duke of Wharton, whose behavior was wildly inconsistent except in betraying a "Lust of Praise." His vanity and self-importance ultimately led him to turn traitor to England. Pope concludes the poem, addressed to Sir Richard Temple, Viscount Cobham, with a flattering counter-assessment: Cobham is known by his ruling passion for the safety of his country.

The Restoration & 18th Century

The genius of the period from 1660 to 1790 did not, frankly, lie in poetry. With the exception of John Dryden (best known for his plays) and Alexander Pope (who gets his own chapter), its great writers were greater in prose than in verse. It was a very analytical, very formal, very prosy age whose ideals were best expressed in essays, satires, and the brand new genre of the novel. Many of the big names—Bunyan, Defoe, Addison, Steele, and Boswell—wrote no poetry to speak of. And those that did—such as Samuel Johnson and Jonathan Swift—aren't remembered for it.

The poets included in this chapter are all minor figures, though they were well enough known in the 18th and 19th centuries to become quotable. They are:

SAMUEL BUTLER (1612–1680): a savage satirist of the recently defeated Puritan revolutionaries; his mock-heroic *Hudibras* was one of King Charles II's favorite books;

THOMAS GRAY (1716–1771): a reclusive Cambridge professor who became the most popular poet of the 1740s and '50s; his "Elegy Written in a Country Churchyard" is perhaps the all-time favorite poem of the 18th century;

WILLIAM COWPER (1731–1800): a dysfunctionally depressive invalid who sought relief by writing thousands and thousands of verses, all but a few now forgotten; began his major work, *The Task,* when a lady suggested he write about a sofa.

As for Dryden, his most quoted line—"Dead men tell no tales"—appears in a play (*The Spanish Friar*) and he quotes it as a proverb.

To Look a Gift Horse in the Mouth

His knowledge was not far behind
The knight's, but of another kind,
And he another way came by it;
Some call it *Gift,* and some *New-Light,*
A liberal art, that costs no pains
Of study, industry, or brains.
His wits were sent him for a token,
But in the carriage cracked and broken....
He ne'er considered it, as loth
To look a gift-horse in the mouth;
And very wisely would lay forth
No more upon it than 'twas worth.

Samuel Butler, *Hudibras,* Part I (1663),
Canto I, 477–84, 487–90

With *Hudibras* Samuel Butler attempted to write the English *Don Quixote.* He failed.

On the other hand, he first recorded the canonical version of the phrase "to look a gift horse in the mouth." (The now-unquoted "Look a *given* horse in the mouth" is earlier.) The allusion is to the practice of examining a horse's teeth to determine its age—a fine thing to do if you're buying it, but rude if you're given it. (The modern equivalent would be to check for a price tag.)

The gift horse in this case is the wit of Ralph, Sir Hudibras's squire and Pancho to his Quixote. Ralph is "gifted" with a certain natural knowledge—which Butler snidely likens to "New Light," the Puritans' term for divine inspiration. Ralph's gift was slightly damaged in transit (*carriage*), but he takes what he can get, not looking this gift horse in the mouth.

The basic idea of the "gift horse" traces at least to the writings of St. Jerome, who coined the Latin version. Its first English appearance was in John Stanbridge's 1520 collection of *Vulgaria* ("Common Sayings"): "A given horse may not be looked in the teeth."

Ignorance Is Bliss

To each his sufferings: all are men,
　　Condemned alike to groan;
The tender for another's pain,
　　The unfeeling for his own.
Yet ah! why should they know their fate?
Since sorrow never comes too late,
　　And happiness too swiftly flies.
Thought would destroy their paradise.
No more; where ignorance is bliss,
　　'Tis folly to be wise.

Thomas Gray, "Ode on a Distant Prospect of
Eton College" (1742), 91–100

❧

This morose ode's epigraph pretty well sums up its theme: "I am man, a sufficient reason to be miserable." It is also typical of Thomas Gray (1716–1771), a melancholic recluse who rarely left the grounds of Eton College, Cambridge, where he was educated and later held a chair in history.

The poem neatly divides into two five-stanza halves. In the first, Gray describes the beauty of Eton's grounds and the frolicsome ways of its undergrads, who study and play and blithely seek adventure. The second half is the bring-down. "Alas," Gray writes, "regardless of their doom, / The little victims play!" Little do they know they're ultimately bound for a life of misfortune, anger, fear, heartbreak, jealousy, envy, despair, scorn, infamy, and several more stanzas' worth of hideous ills, culminating in poverty, sickness, and death.

On the evidence of this poem, it's probably a good thing Professor Gray had little contact with Eton's student body. He admits in the end that the young are entitled to their ignorance, which as he famously said "is bliss," but that didn't stop him from publishing the ode.

Though Gray's assessment was popular then and remains oft-repeated, writers have argued the point since the heyday of ancient Greece. Sophocles, for example, anticipated Gray in the tragedy *Ajax*: "In knowing nothing is the sweetest life." Euripides also weighed in on the side of bliss in his play *Antiope*: "Ignorance of one's misfortunes is clear gain." The Roman poet Ovid agreed in *The Art of Love*: "It is well for men to be ignorant of many things." Similar sentiments appear in numerous English poems by the likes of William Cowper, Thomas Hood, and Matthew Prior ("From ignorance our comfort flows").

More numerous, however, are contrary claims. No less authoritative a source than the Talmud warns that "Ignorance and conceit go hand in hand." Samuel Butler (of "gift horse" fame) echoes the sentiment: "The truest characters of ignorance / Are vanity, and pride, and arrogance." The satirist Thersites in Shakespeare's *Troilus and Cressida* calls "folly and ignorance" the "common curse of mankind," while Feste notes in *Twelfth Night* that "There is no darkness but ignorance." Perhaps the final word, and the most crushing blow to Gray's theory, is the observation by pioneer sociologist Herbert Spencer that "Our lives are universally shortened by our ignorance."

Far from the Madding Crowd

> Far from the madding crowd's ignoble strife,
>   Their sober wishes never learned to stray;
> Along the cool sequestered vale of life
>   They kept the noiseless tenor of their way.
>
> Gray, "Elegy Written in a Country
>   Churchyard" (1749), 73–76

It's certain this line would be much less famous if Thomas Hardy hadn't stolen it, but Gray's "Elegy" remains one of the most widely taught English poems.

Like Gray's Eton ode (page 128), the elegy is morbid, but much better at it and less clichéd to boot. Left blissfully alone at dusk in a quiet country graveyard—far from the annoying bustle of happy students—Gray is able to peacefully meditate. And where in the ode signs of joy and life made him think of sorrow and death, in the elegy signs of death elicit thoughts of life's little joys.

His basic point is that we shouldn't scorn the brief, obscure lives of simple country folk, as if a life without achievement or glory is somehow less a life. What's the value of wealth, fame, honor, beauty, praise, or prizes once we're in the ground? "Can Honor's voice provoke the silent dust, / Or Flattery soothe the dull cold ear of Death?"

Furthermore, how can we judge the true worth of those whose remains are marked only by humble stones? Perhaps among them lies one as great as those who were famous—"Some mute inglorious Milton here may rest, / Some Cromwell guiltless of his country's blood."

In fact, both the greatest and most horrible men are guided partly by circumstance: accidents of birth, chance opportunities, pure luck. Simple men who lead simple, obscure, and largely virtuous lives have simply never been tempted to live otherwise. They live beyond the influence of the "madding crowd" that lures men from the right Godly path to a simple Godly death.

Which is all well and good; but what does *madding* mean? Not "maddening," though that would make sense here, but "increasingly mad"—i.e., in the grip of a self-perpetuating frenzy. Spenser used the word first in *The Shepheardes Calender* (1579); but Gray's model was probably this line from a 1614 work by the minor poet William Drummond of Hawthornden: "Far from the madding Worldling's hoarse discords."

God Moves in Mysterious Ways

God moves in a mysterious way,
  His wonders to perform;
He plants his footsteps in the sea,
  And rides upon the storm.

Deep in unfathomable mines
  Of never failing skill,
He treasures up his bright designs,
  And works his sov'reign will.

Ye fearful saints, fresh courage take;
  The clouds ye so much dread
Are big with mercy, and shall break
  In blessings on your head.

William Cowper, "Light Shining Out of
Darkness" (1772), 1–12

For the better part of his life, poet William Cowper (pronounced *Cooper*) struggled with terrible fits of depression, which reduced him at times to an invalid. In the aftermath of one attack, he embraced Evangelical Christianity, an emotional faith stressing personal relations with the Savior. But in the aftermath of another, he became convinced that he was eternally damned, and that he could have no relations with the Savior, personal or otherwise.

It was on the verge of this second attack, while there was still hope, that Cowper wrote "Light Shining Out of Darkness," one of 66 pieces he contributed to a collection of Evangelical hymns. Many of Cowper's hymns assess the evils and pains of mortal existence; sometimes he concludes that these "storms" are the work of Satan, other times that they're tests of faith. Here he concludes that we cannot really grasp their reason, for "God moves in a mysterious way."

We say "ways," which slightly distorts Cowper's meaning. For however many are His wonders and purposes, and however contradictory His works on Earth, God's way is ultimately whole and one—we're just incapable of discerning it. All we can do is believe in His providence, which will be revealed to us in the hereafter. Or rather, it will be revealed to his "saints," by which Cowper means those souls who make it to heaven. Within a year Cowper would despair of joining their company, convinced that he would never know the blessings of God, or the mystery of His way.

Variety's the Spice of Life

Variety's the very spice of life
That gives it all its flavor. We have run
Through ev'ry change that fancy at the loom
Exhausted, has had genius to supply,
And studious of mutation still, discard
A real elegance little used,
For monstrous novelty and strange disguise.

Cowper, *The Task* (1785), Book II, 606–12

This phrase, which we take seriously now, was held in contempt by the poet who coined it. Variety may lend our life its flavor, but in Cowper's opinion that only proves how sadly lost we are.

Cowper wrote *The Task,* a massive poem in blank verse, to distract himself from his crushing depression. Its title refers to many things, among them the duty of Christian people to discern God's will and live a life of simple virtue. In Book II, Cowper continues a long tradition in English poetry of accusing the clergy of corruption, impotence, and neglecting its flock.

One result is chronic dissatisfaction and emptiness, perfectly symptomized by the rabid consumerism and fashion frenzy of the London elite. The city gentleman's guide isn't his pastor, but his tailor; and with every change of the moon he changes his wardrobe. The garment industry can't keep up; and the perfectly suitable garments of old are discarded for "monstrous novelty and strange disguise."

So this is what "variety" amounts to: a mindless, directionless grasping after novelty. Coming at the expense of "household joys / And comforts," replacing "peace and hospitality" with "hunger, frost, and woe," it's a bitter spice indeed. Cowper prefers the simple, unaffected country life, with its comforting lack of variety, the soothing sameness that he hoped would keep him from going completely insane.

William Wordsworth

Keats wrote more beautifully, and Byron was more fun, but William Wordsworth (1770–1850) has gone down in history as *the* major Romantic poet. He outlived all the others, which helped; but his reputation rests mostly on his clear expression of Romantic principles and his influence not only on peers but on subsequent generations.

Often plain, Wordsworth's verse is also remarkably honest and pure; he took poetic self-expression to a new level. His plainness and sincerity were in fact revolutionary, a blow against the obscurity and artificiality of most contemporary verse. Though his work was initially greeted with hostility by the critics and most of his fellow poets, it soon became inescapable.

Wordsworth's revolutionary pursuit of a poetry about and for the common man was initially inspired by revolutionary politics. While sojourning in France in 1791–1792, he embraced the democratic ideals of the French Revolution. However, once he returned home and England declared war against France, he began to reconsider. Revolted by Robespierre's Reign of Terror, he renounced his youthful politics; however, his poetic credo remained democratic. With his new friend Samuel Taylor Coleridge, he published the groundbreaking *Lyrical Ballads* in 1798, and they subsequently collaborated on the famous preface to that work (the actual composition was Wordsworth's).

Wordsworth's masterwork, *The Prelude,* finished in 1805 but published only posthumously, provides the

❧

details of Wordsworth's physical and psychological journeys in the 1790s and 1800s. It's a searching work of epic proportions, though it takes true stamina to get through. Most readers will prefer his lyrics and odes of the period, which include the great "Tintern Abbey" and "Intimations of Immortality."

The critical hostility toward Wordsworth gradually turned to admiration, and from the 1810s on he lived an increasingly comfortable and rewarding life in England's famous Lake District (which he and his sister Dorothy helped make famous). At the same time, his poetry lost much of its fire, leaving it often dull and prosaic. Few readers now bother with his other epic-length work, *The Excursion* (1814), or the increasingly minor verse of his later years. Wordsworth's poetry became safe, and as a reward he was named England's poet laureate in 1843, seven years before his death.

Emotion Recollected in Tranquillity

[Each of the poems in these volumes] has a worthy *purpose*. Not that I always began to write with a distinct purpose formally con_.ived; but habits of meditation have, I trust, so prompted and regulated my feelings that my descriptions of such objects as strongly excite those feelings will be found to carry along with them a *purpose*. If this opinion be erroneous, I can have little right to the name of poet. For all good poetry is the spontaneous overflow of powerful feelings....

I have said that poetry is the spontaneous overflow of powerful feelings; it takes its origin from

emotion recollected in tranquillity: the emotion is
contemplated till, by a species of reaction, the
tranquillity gradually disappears, and an emotion,
kindred to that which was before the subject of
contemplation, is gradually produced, and does
itself actually exist in the mind. In this mood successful composition generally begins....

Preface to the Second Edition of
Lyrical Ballads, revised (1802)

Lyrical Ballads, a collection of poems by Wordsworth and
S. T. Coleridge, was first published anonymously in 1798,
but Wordsworth was too immodest to remain anonymous
once the volume took off. In the second edition of 1800
he not only revealed his name but also added a slew of
new poems plus a prefatory manifesto. It was in this preface as much as in the poems that followed that the
Romantic movement began.

Although not entirely unprecedented, *Lyrical Ballads*
was quite different from the poetical works of earlier
periods. There had been poetry in a high style, written in
an elevated and copiously adorned language; and there
had been poetry in a low style, such as popular ballads
and lyrics, plain but also emotionally coarse. Wordsworth
and Coleridge aimed for the middle: high feelings
expressed in plain language.

In his preface, Wordsworth takes a fair amount of
credit for this new "Romantic" style of poetry, neglecting
to mention the refreshing work of earlier contemporaries
such as Burns and Blake—let alone much older poets
such as Michael Drayton, who wrote lovely and moving
Renaissance lyrics. On the other hand, Wordsworth and
Coleridge had a far greater impact on the future of Eng-

lish poetry than the idiosyncratic Blake and the dialectical Burns, and Wordsworth set out his principles with precision and clarity.

All good poetry, according to Wordsworth, "is the spontaneous overflow of powerful feelings." But good poetry isn't spewed out in the heat of an emotional moment; it is the eruption of feelings that have distilled for a time in the mind, now clearer and more refined than when they were first felt. So by *spontaneous* he doesn't really mean "spontaneous," except insofar as a feeling can be spontaneously felt twice, in its first heat and in its later refinement.

That is, the basis of such poetry is "emotion recollected in tranquillity," away from the confusion and distraction of the initial moment. The spontaneous part is capturing this recollection as it arises, in the plain language of the heart, without belaboring it or gussying it up with far-fetched figures of speech. And while plain, it is still *purposive,* meaning that it presents feelings in relation to one another, revealing through such relations "what is really important to men." In other words, while poetry like Wordsworth's may seem simple, unsophisticated, or naively emotional, it's really very important.

Wordsworth admits that he's not full of much "false modesty." It almost makes you hate to admit how great his best work is.

~∞~

Little, Nameless, Unremembered Acts of Kindness and of Love

These beauteous forms,
Through a long absence, have not been to me
As is a landscape to a blind man's eye;
But oft, in lonely rooms, and 'mid the din
Of towns and cities, I have owed to them,
In hours of weariness, sensations sweet,
Felt in the blood, and felt among the heart;
And passing even into my purer mind,
With tranquil restoration—feelings too
Of unremembered pleasure; such, perhaps,
As have no slight or trivial influence
On that best portion of a good man's life,
His little, nameless, unremembered acts
Of kindness and of love.

"Lines Composed a Few Miles above
Tintern Abbey" (1798), 22–35

"Tintern Abbey," the last poem in *Lyrical Ballads,* is set in a cottage above the River Wye in Monmouthshire. Wordsworth is on one of his famous walking tours, and as he reposes under a tranquil sycamore he recalls his last visit to the spot, five years before. Seeing the landscape again, with its little hedgerows, its groves, orchards, and copses, revives the feelings he felt on his first view, feelings which have in the interim been distilled in his "purer mind."

Not all these feelings arise from conscious memories. Some arise from forgotten pleasures, opaque to the inner eye, but no less influential than remembered pleasures. Wordsworth figures that these subtler influences have quietly bettered his character: Small doses of natural purity have inspired equally small, but equally pure, "little nameless, unremembered acts / Of kindness and of love."

This resonant phrase has a history akin to those forgotten pleasures; though rarely quoted in full, it is the ancestor of numberless descriptions of selfless beneficence. (Practically every writer has at some point read "Tintern Abbey.") The best-known recent version is the somewhat fatuous slogan, "Practice random kindness and senseless acts of beauty," coined by Marin County housesitter Anne Herbert.

The Child Is Father of the Man

> My heart leaps up when I behold
>   A rainbow in the sky:
> So was it when my life began;
> So is it now I am a man;
> So be it when I shall grow old,
>   Or let me die!
> The Child is father of the Man;
> And I could wish my days to be
> Bound each to each in natural piety.
>
> "My Heart Leaps Up" (1802)

This, like virtually all Wordsworth's lyrics, is a far cry from the poetry familiar to most of his original readers, which was generally either overwrought or underthought.

In his preface to *Lyrical Ballads*, Wordsworth defines a poet as "a man speaking to men," superior in sensibility but not therefore required to write unnatural language.

Versus the "gaudiness and inane trivialities" of what many mistook for poetry, Wordsworth strove to write simply but feelingly about common human experiences.

None of his poems better exemplifies this aim than "My Heart Leaps Up." It's a simple and straightforward description of a universal feeling: awe at the sight of a rainbow. The speaker exults in the feeling and would rather die than ever lose his capacity to be awed anew by nature's simple wonders. He wishes, at the end, for daily experience of such "natural piety," the sense that a higher power is revealed in nature.

As simple (or simple-minded) as the poem is, it does contain one brief figurative turn, the paradoxical seventh line: "The Child is father of the Man." The capital letters are a clue that Wordsworth means "Child" and "Man" allegorically. What he's getting at is that childhood feelings—such as natural awe—give birth to the mature feelings that succeed them as we age.

The World Is Too Much with Us
and Getting and Spending

> The world is too much with us; late and soon,
> Getting and spending, we lay waste our powers;
> Little we see in Nature that is ours;
> We have given our hearts away, a sordid boon!
> This Sea that bares her bosom to the moon,
> The winds that will be howling at all hours,
> And are up-gathered now like sleeping flowers,
> For this, for everything, we are out of tune;
> It moves us not—Great God! I'd rather be

A Pagan suckled in a creed outworn;
So might I, standing on this pleasant lea,
Have glimpses that would make me less forlorn;
Have sight of Proteus rising from the sea;
Or hear old Triton blow his wreathéd horn.

"The World Is Too Much with Us" (1807)

This sonnet makes an interesting companion to "My Heart Leaps Up" (page 140). In that poem Wordsworth celebrates his capacity to be awed by nature; in this he rues others' deficiency.

Coining two phrases in the first two lines, Wordsworth complains that the "world is too much with us" and that we're too caught up in "getting and spending." The second part is clear enough: We busy ourselves with material gain when we ought to be communing with the flowers and trees in a state of natural piety.

But aren't flowers and trees also part of the "world"? And isn't gold produced by nature? Wordsworth's terms are a little fuzzy; in *world* he seems to include only those things (man-made *or* natural) which distract us from the spiritual. Nevertheless, it's a world we need to deal with; his complaint is that we squander our spiritual powers by dealing *only* with that world.

Alternatively, we can read the line with a stress on "too much with us": Even if *world* includes the world of nature, we consume it as if it were merely an inert resource, rather than letting it work on our spirit and lead us *beyond* the world to a higher realm of experience. That is, we see the world as separate and spiritless, rather than as an expression of a higher spirit we share in.

In "My Heart Leaps Up," Wordsworth says he would rather die than lose his heart and be unmoved by rainbows. This time the alternative is less radical: He'd rather be a pagan, like the ancient Greeks and Romans. They at least could appreciate the divine power present in the sea, even if this power took the form of false gods like Proteus and Triton. He prefers their fear and awe to Christian indifference.

The Romantic Period

Conventionally dated from the 1790s to the 1830s, the Romantic Period is one of the great eras of English lyric poetry. The name "Romantic" doesn't mean that all these lyrics are love poems—few are. The term derives from 18th-century German philosophy and refers to a move away from the Enlightenment values of rationalism, analysis, and wit. The new philosophers and poets sought a more emotional, more "natural" expression of the human condition, and they turned to common wisdom and common experience for their values. If the poetry of the Enlightenment—such as Pope's—had been urbane and elitist, the poetry of the Romantics was relatively simple and natural.

Of course, not every English poet who wrote in the early 19th century subscribed to German philosophy or even to the program set forth in Wordsworth and Coleridge's *Lyrical Ballads,* which defined the Romantic "movement" (page 136). In one way or another, though, the poets in this chapter saw their work as a break with the past, and there was plenty of mutual influence to go around. These poets are:

ROBERT BURNS (1759–1796): a Scottish farmer who revived the tradition of local folktale and ballad; wrote mostly in Scots dialect; now commonly and annoyingly nicknamed "Bobbie";

WILLIAM BLAKE (1757–1827): a London artist, engraver, and printer whose passionately unorthodox and visionary poems were all but ignored in his day; created a whole big complicated symbolic system you need a guidebook to penetrate; liked to walk around his house naked;

SAMUEL TAYLOR COLERIDGE (1772–1834): collaborator and friend of Wordsworth, opium addict, and leading English proponent of German Romantic philosophy;

SIR WALTER SCOTT (1771–1832): a "Romantic" mostly in that his works are inspired by old heroic romances; when the public tired of his poems he turned his efforts to novels, which today are better known;

GEORGE GORDON, LORD BYRON (1788–1824): whose racy narrative poems became more popular than Scott's, but whose alleged libertinism forced him into Italian exile with his friends Percy and Mary Shelley;

JOHN KEATS (1795–1821): now considered the most brilliant of all Romantic poets, though his career was tragically brief; wrote beautiful letters too.

The other great poet of the period was Percy Bysshe Shelley, whose poems are great but almost never quoted. His most famous line—in which he defines poets as the "unacknowledged legislators of the world"—appears in an essay.

The Best-Laid Plans of Mice and Men

Thou saw the fields laid bare and waste,
An' weary winter comin' fast,
An' cozie here, beneath the blast,
    Thou thought to dwell,
Till crash! the cruel coulter passed
    Out-through thy cell....

But Mousie, thou art no thy lane,
In proving foresight may be vain:
The best-laid schemes o' mice an' men
    Gang aft a-gley,
An' lea'e us nought but grief an' pain,
    For promised joy.

Robert Burns, "To a Mouse" (1785),
25–30, 37–42

There's a nice lilt to Burns' original Scots—"The best-laid schemes o' mice an' men / Gang aft a-gley"—but whoever converted it to standard English did the phrase a big favor. He or she could have left "schemes" alone, but few outside Scotland would know what to do with "Gang aft a-gley."

Gang, though rare even in Scottish writings, isn't hard to grasp: It's just dialect for "go"; *aft* is simply a variant of *oft.* *A-gley* is stranger, having no English cousins and being based on the equally obscure verb *glee,* "squint, look sideways." The suggestion of a sideways or off-center perspective explains how *a-gley* came to mean "askew" or "awry." In fact, *awry* is a similar construction, based on the adjective *wry,* which originally meant "skewed" or "twisted."

❧

That we quote a comprehensible English version rather than the original Scots is itself a scheme gone a-gley. Burns didn't write in dialect by chance; it was part of a deliberate attempt to craft poetry about and for regular Scottish country folk. By profession Burns was himself a country farmer, though also a widely learned man perfectly capable of writing standard English.

Another part of the scheme was to make poems out of simple everyday happenings, such as Burns's upturning a mouse's nest with his *coulter,* or plowshare. This poem is his recompense, an apology and a consolation. Burns is sorry to have destroyed the mouse's shelter against the oncoming "weary winter." But he urges the mouse not to feel too bad, since it's not alone (*no thy lane*) in having its plans go awry.

If I were the mouse, I'm not sure I'd be satisfied. There's a bit of a difference between plans falling through and plans being wrecked. Burns is like someone who burns your house down and then tells you, "These things happen."

Auld Lang Syne

> Should auld acquaintance be forgot,
>   And never brought to min'?
> Should auld acquaintance be forgot,
>   And days o' lang syne?
>
> For auld lang syne, my dear,
>   For auld lang syne,
> We'll tak a cup o' kindness yet,
>   For auld lang syne.

Burns, "Auld Lang Syne" (1788), 1–8

∿ↄↄ

Burns had no intention of writing a New Year's song when he composed this rousing (or carousing) number. It's a more all-purpose drinking song, the kind aging buddies sing in maudlin moments down at the pub.

Auld lang syne means literally "old long since," as in "when we were young." The singers bid each other to recall the days when they ran about the *braes* (hillsides) picking daisies, and when they paddled in the *burns* (streams) from morning to noon. They've wandered many a weary foot since then, and seas have roared between them; but despite time and tide they can still relive the jolly days of youth over a "cup o' kindness" (friendship).

Note that Burns didn't write "And days of auld lang syne," which is how today's revelers tend to sing it, or slur it. The word *days* gets a full two beats, not just a beat and a half. The original tune, furthermore, is five times as long as the verse and chorus quoted here, which makes it considerably less monotonous than the version sung over and over and over as the corks are popping.

Little Lamb, Who Made Thee?

Little Lamb, who made thee?
Dost thou know who made thee?
Gave thee life & bid thee feed,
By the stream & o'er the mead;
Gave thee clothing of delight,
Softest clothing wooly bright;
Gave thee such a tender voice,
Making all the vales rejoice!
Little Lamb who made thee?
Dost thou know who made thee?

〜〜

Little Lamb I'll tell thee,
  Little Lamb I'll tell thee!
He is called by thy name,
For he calls himself a Lamb:
He is meek & he is mild,
He became a little child;
I a child & thou a lamb,
We are called by his name.
  Little Lamb God bless thee.
  Little Lamb God bless thee.

William Blake, *Songs of Innocence* (1789),
"The Lamb"

William Blake (1757–1827) is much admired today—
especially for his *Songs of Innocence* (1789) and *Songs of
Experience* (1794). But he was not widely read until this
century; and despite his profound influence on certain
poets, he has left only a few impressions on English
speech.

Even today Blake's work is seldom read the way he
intended. Beginning with *Songs of Innocence,* his second
book, Blake published his work in a series of hand-
engraved, hand-colored, and hand-bound "plates" combining text and illustration. "The Lamb," best-known of
the *Innocence* poems, shows a little country boy outside a
thatched barn addressing one of a flock of lambs; the
lamb gazes up with a meek, inquisitive look.

The text of the poem comprises the boy's questions
and instructions to the lamb. "Little Lamb, who made
thee?" asks the boy; when the lamb fails to respond, he
reveals the answer. It was God who made the lamb, and
who gave it a soft white coat and a tender voice—God,

who became the child Jesus, who compared himself to a lamb (John 1:29, etc.).

The child's view of God's miraculous works is typical of the book, which embodies an innocent, untroubled view of nature and society. Blake celebrates this view, but at the same time he presents it as incomplete. Some of the *Innocence* poems, such as "The Chimney Sweeper," reveal a hard, tragic reality behind the naive perceptions. Blake would provide a balancing counterpart to innocence in *Songs of Experience,* added on five years later, in which a tiger takes the lamb's place.

Fearful Symmetry

Tyger Tyger, burning bright,
In the forests of the night;
What immortal hand or eye,
Could frame thy fearful symmetry?

In what distant deeps or skies
Burnt the fire of thine eyes?
On what wings dare he aspire?
What the hand, dare seize the fire?

And what shoulder, & what art,
Could twist the sinews of thy heart?
And when thy heart began to beat,
What dread hand? & what dread feet?

What the hammer? what the chain,
In what furnace was thy brain?
What the anvil? what dread grasp,
Dare its deadly terrors clasp!

When the stars threw down their spears
And water'd heaven with their tears:
Did he smile his work to see?
Did he who made the Lamb make thee?

Tyger Tyger burning bright,
In the forests of the night:
What immortal hand or eye,
Dare frame thy fearful symmetry?

Blake, *Songs of Experience* (1794), "The Tyger"

Speaking of symmetry, you'll notice strong parallels between this poem and "The Lamb" (page 148). Like that poem, "The Tyger" (an archaic spelling) begins by asking the beast a question; in fact it's the same question: Who made you? The answer in both cases is the same (God),

but not the same—the creator of "The Tyger" is very different from the creator of "The Lamb."

We don't know who's addressing the tiger—Blake's engraving shows only the animal (and actually he looks sort of cuddly). Whoever the speaker, he or she is a lot less naive than the boy of "The Lamb." This speaker knows fear, and fears the tiger, and by extension fears the God who could have made so dangerous a creature. The lamb-child Jesus of the earlier poem is replaced here by a deity akin to the Greek god Hephaestus, a god of fire and metal who grasps and twists and beats dark forces into a terrible shape.

This is the God of the Book of Job (which Blake would later illustrate), responsible for such awful monsters as Behemoth and Leviathan, and responsible as well for Job's cruel and senseless suffering. Blake knew the Bible well, and claimed to draw all his inspiration from it; he knew it too well to hold a naive, uncomplicated view of God, who is fearful and punishing as well as nurturing and good.

"Fearful symmetry" is the speaker's most memorable and suggestive phrase. (It is also the title of Northrop Frye's well-known study of Blake.) It is not only the tiger's power and danger that inspire fear; it's also the fact that a creature so dangerous could be so perfectly crafted. The tiger wasn't an accident of nature: God clearly took some care in making it. Its symmetry proves it was *intentional,* and that's the scariest part.

The Doors of Perception

The ancient tradition that the world will be consumed in fire at the end of six thousand years is true. as I have heard from Hell.

For the cherub with his flaming sword is hereby commanded to leave his guard at the tree of life, and when he does, the whole creation will be consumed, and appear infinite. and holy whereas it now appears finite & corrupt.

This will come to pass by an improvement of sensual enjoyment.

But first the notion that man has a body distinct from his soul, is to be expunged; this I shall do, by printing in the infernal method, by corrosives, which in Hell are salutary and medicinal, melting apparent surfaces away, and displaying the infinite which was hid.

If the doors of perception were cleansed every thing would appear to man as it is: infinite.

For man has closed himself up, till he sees all things thro' narrow chinks of his cavern.

Blake, *The Marriage of Heaven and Hell* (1793), plate 14 [Blake's punctuation]

Combining verse and prose, Blake's *Marriage of Heaven and Hell* is characteristically idiosyncratic, contrarian, satirical, and defiant. Blake proudly proclaims himself a partisan of Hell, or what repressive, orthodox Christians call Hell. In Blake's view, their simplistic notions of good and evil are delusional and unhealthy, splitting man's God-given nature into separate and supposedly antithetical parts—body and soul, passion and reason.

Blake outright rejected the belief system of his sanctimonious contemporaries, replacing it with a complicated and often arcane system of his own. As he saw it, traditional views of good and evil are not just false, they're harmful. "Prisons are built with stones of Law, Brothels with bricks of Religion" he writes in the *Marriage*. Social ills arise from human attempts to stigmatize and repress what is natural; when bound by artificial strictures, the natural becomes corrupted.

Blake hoped to burn away these false beliefs with his poetry, in which he embraced and applied the corrosive energies of "Hell." He proclaimed that his biting satire, which orthodox opinion might call "infernal," was just good medicine. He likewise explains that his use of acid in making printing plates is symbolically a blow against a corrupt society. (He engraved, painted, and printed his poems himself.)

Blake believed that he could thus cleanse "the doors of perception." These are not the five senses, which are mere "chinks" in a dark cavern of dualistic thought, allowing in only finite sensations. Blake believed that we're capable of perceiving far more; if we free our minds from false divisions, if we learn to see with both body and soul, we will be able to grasp the "infinite and holy."

Blake's poetry may have worked for some people, but it certainly hasn't had very widespread effects—those traditional notions of good and evil and heaven and hell are very much alive and well. Others have sought more effective cleansers for the doors of perception—notably Aldous Huxley, who stole Blake's phrase for the title of a book on mescaline.

An Albatross around Your Neck

The ice was here, the ice was there,
The ice was all around:
It cracked and growled, and roared and howled,
Like noises in a swound!

At length did cross an Albatross,
Thorough the fog it came;
As if it had been a Christian soul,
We hailed it in God's name.

It ate the food it ne'er had eat,
And round and round it flew.
The ice did split with thunder-fit;
The helmsman steered us through!

Samuel Taylor Coleridge, *The Rime of the
Ancient Mariner* (1798), 59–70

In an essay on Shakespeare, Coleridge wrote that Iago, in the tragedy *Othello,* acts not from a conscious motive, but from a "motiveless malignity." In other words, he was bad for no good reason.

"Motiveless malignity" also applies to the Ancient Mariner who narrates Coleridge's poem. According to his tale, he set out as a younger mariner on a ship bound south. When the ship reached the equator, a strange uncanny storm descended, blowing it thousands of miles off course into a God-forsaken sea of ice.

There was nothing the ship could do, until an albatross flew by. According to seafaring superstition, albatrosses (huge white birds) embodied the souls of sailors lost at sea; they were also omens of good luck. And indeed this albatross does bring luck, as the ice breaks up and the ship sails free. In the following days, the bird follows the ship on its way back north.

But then, for no good reason at all, the mariner shoots the bird dead with his crossbow. Perhaps the devil made him do it, but whatever the cause, the result was disaster. An evil spirit pursues the ship and stalls it, until fresh water runs out. The sea begins to crawl with "slimy things" (a brood of water-snakes) and to burn with "death-fires" (St. Elmo's fire). The rest of the crew naturally blame the mariner, and as a sign of his guilt they hang the corpse of the albatross around his neck. Thus was born the symbol of a burdensome curse, passed down to generations of students.

A Ghastly Crew

They groaned, they stirred, they all uprose,
Nor spake, nor moved their eyes;
It had been strange, even in a dream,
To have seen those dead men rise.

The helmsman steered, the ship moved on;
Yet never a breeze up-blew;
The mariners all 'gan work the ropes,
Where they were wont to do;
They raised their limbs like lifeless tools—
We were a ghastly crew.

Coleridge, *The Rime of the Ancient Mariner,*
331–40

We use "ghastly crew" for a merely repulsive group; the Ancient Mariner, who coins the phrase, is speaking more literally.

Ghastly derives from the Old English verb *gast,* "frighten, terrify," which in turn gave rise to the noun *ghost,* "frightening thing." Until after Coleridge's day, *ghastly* always referred to something truly horrifying, rather than merely awful. Coleridge really means "ghastly crew": dead sailors from a lost ship, brought back to life by "ghosts" or spirits.

The crew had died of thirst after their ship was blown to the middle of nowhere and left without wind or rain. The Mariner, who by killing an albatross caused the whole ordeal (page 155), is the only survivor—apparently all those deaths were meant to teach him a lesson. When he repents and learns to love God's creatures, the albatross falls off his neck, a rain begins to fall, and "a troop of spirits blest" take charge of the ship.

It's thus by God's grace that he lives to tell the tale. On the other hand, he must continue to pay for his crime by telling the tale forever to those who need to hear it:

> I pass, like night, from land to land;
> I have strange power of speech;
> That moment that his face I see,
> I know the man that must hear me:
> To him my tale I teach. (586–90)

All Things Both Great and Small *and* Sadder but Wiser

Farewell, farewell! but this I tell
To thee, thou Wedding Guest!
He prayeth well, who loveth well
Both man and bird and beast.

He prayeth best, who loveth best
All things both great and small;
For the dear God who loveth us,
He made and loveth all.

The Mariner, whose eye is bright,
Whose beard with age is hoar,
Is gone: and now the Wedding Guest
Turned from the bridegroom's door.

He went like one that hath been stunned
And is of sense forlorn:
A sadder and a wiser man,
He rose the morrow morn.

Coleridge, *The Rime of the Ancient Mariner,*
610–25

The "Wedding Guest"—accosted outside a church—has listened to the Ancient Mariner's tale with a sick fascination, unable to break away. He's heard the grim fate of the Mariner's ship, whose entire crew of 200 men drop dead. He's heard of bizarre supernatural visitations from such characters as Life-in-Death and a thousand thousand slimy water snakes. He's heard how spirits inhabited the ship-men's corpses, guiding the boat back home. And finally he's heard of the Mariner's rescue and shriving by a Hermit of the Wood.

And what is the lesson of this horrifying tale? "He prayeth best, who loveth best / All things both great and small." This simple bit of wisdom, though well suited to a country veterinarian, seems a little inadequate to account for the death and destruction the Mariner has related.

But the Mariner's gripping tale is meant to be an old-fashioned allegory, allowing for large doses of hyperbole and symbolism. Coleridge's point is not only that all living things are dear to God—so killing is a grave offense—but also that the spiritual world is continuous with the natural world. To strike out at nature is to invite unforeseen and perhaps disastrous spiritual results.

This is the knowledge that leaves the Wedding Guest "a sadder and a wiser man"—a phrase which is the direct ancestor of the modern saying "sadder but wiser." By changing Coleridge's *and* to *but,* we imply that sorrow and wisdom are contraries, but the poet knew better. The Mariner's sorrowful tale teaches the Guest things he was happier not to know, leaving him less blissfully ignorant of life's mysterious wholeness.

Obviously, the Mariner's lesson, like the poem as a whole, is more difficult for the reader than for the Guest to swallow. The *Rime* is rather baroque and fantastic, but for Coleridge the challenge was to make the fantastic credible. As he wrote in *Biographia Literaria* (1817), his aim was to take "persons and characters supernatural" and to lend them "a human interest and a semblance of truth sufficient to procure for these shadows of imagination that willing suspension of disbelief for the moment, which constitutes poetic faith." ("Suspension of disbelief" was coined in this passage.) To succeed, the poem must carry you away, which depends both on the poem's power and on your own willingness to believe it. In this sense, skepticism is the enemy of poetic wisdom.

To Beard the Lion in His Den

> On the earl's cheek the flush of rage
> O'ercame the ashen hue of age:
> Fierce he broke forth,—"And darest thou then
> To beard the lion in his den,
>   The Douglas in his hall?"

> Sir Walter Scott, *Marmion* (1808),
> Canto VI, stanza xiv

The "Douglas" of Sir Walter Scott's romance *Marmion* is Archibald Douglas, Fifth Earl of Angus (1449–1514), a famously fiery character and Scottish national hero. His main claim to literary fame, besides siring the poet Gawain Douglas, was that he figured in two animal phrases.

In this passage Douglas, by way of Scott, coins the first. He's rebuking the equally fiery Marmion, an English lord sent as ambassador during the Scottish/English conflict of 1514. (For more on Marmion, see the next entry.) When Douglas refuses to shake the Englishman's hand

and basically calls him slime, Marmion explodes in a rage and reaches for his sword. This prompts Douglas's retort.

"To beard" has at times meant both "to grow a beard" and "to strip one off," with the latter taking on the additional sense of "to emasculate." "No man so potent breathes upon the ground," wrote Shakespeare, "But I will beard him" (*King Henry IV, Part I*; the speaker is another Douglas, Archibald's ancestor). Needless to say, bearding a lion is an especially dangerous feat to attempt; trying to beard one in its very den—on home ground—is even crazier. Marmion doesn't manage it.

The other phrase linked to Douglas is "Bell-the-Cat," which was his nickname. It derives ultimately from a fable by Aesop, in which the mice of a house plot to hang a bell around the neck of their enemy the house cat, so that they might be forewarned of its approach. The problem, though, is that some poor mouse would have to "bell the cat."

The cat in Archibald's day was the hated Earl of Mar, a new-minted aristocrat and favorite of the despised King James III. A group of old nobles gathered to plot Mar's demise; the question, put by Lord Grey, was "Who will bell the cat?" Douglas rose to the challenge, managing to have the Earl captured and hanged. From that day forth Douglas was known as "Bell-the-Cat."

Oh What a Tangled Web We Weave

> Oh! what a tangled web we weave
> When first we practice to deceive!
> A Palmer too!—no wonder why
> I felt rebuked beneath his eye;
> I might have known there was but one
> Whose look could quell Lord Marmion.

Scott, Marmion, Canto VI, stanza xvii

Before he took up writing his great long romantic novels, Sir Walter Scott wrote great long romantic poems, including *The Lay of the Last Minstrel* (1805), *Marmion* (1808), *The Lady of the Lake* (1810), and several others. "Tangled web" is an apt term for them all, *Marmion* in particular, which weaves historical incident into a complex fictional plot in the antique manner of medieval romance.

Scott's tangled plot contains within itself a tangled subplot, devised by the poem's antihero Marmion, a brave but ignoble knight in the service of England's King Henry VIII. Put as simply as possible, Marmion's scheme involves forging evidence of treason against one Sir Ralph de Wilton, whose fiancée (Clare) Marmion covets, even while he maintains an affair with a nun (Constance) disguised as his page.

This is the deception that Marmion *first practices* ("begins to carry out"), and it ultimately spins out of control. His charge against de Wilton is put to trial by combat, with Marmion leaving his rival for dead. De Wilton, however, survives and flees to Scotland, then at war with England, and disguises himself as a palmer

(religious pilgrim). In this guise, and on the eve of the rebellious Scots' disastrous last showdown with England at Flodden Field, de Wilton meets up once more with Marmion and bests him in a second fight, though sparing his life.

In the end, the bad guys (Constance and Marmion) die while the good guys (Clare and de Wilton) are reunited. The moral of the story is that treachery's a sticky business, and that we're likely to get caught in our own webs of deception.

Whom the Gods Love Die Young —

"Whom the gods love die young," was said of
    yore,
  And many deaths do they escape by this:
The death of friends, and that which slays even
    more—
  The death of Friendship, Love, Youth, all that is,
Except mere breath; and since the silent shore
  Awaits at last even those who longest miss
The old Archer's shafts, perhaps the early grave
Which men weep over may be meant to save.

George Gordon, Lord Byron, *Don Juan*
(1818–23), Canto IV, stanza xii

Given his tremendous popularity and his skill in penning witty verses, it's odd that George Gordon, the sixth Lord Byron, contributed so few quotable phrases to English. What's more, one of his two most famous lines is a translation rather than a coinage, as he admits even as he writes it.

In a footnote Byron traces the saying "Whom the gods love die young" to Herodotus, the first Greek historian. I'm not sure where Byron got that idea, since the Greeks themselves thought the comedian Menander coined it in a now lost play from the third or fourth century B.C. Menander's line survived in Classical quote books and popped up again in a comedy by the Roman dramatist Plautus.

Plautus makes fun of the idea, and perhaps so did Menander, which would mean that the line was already a cliché. Byron's version is less obviously satirical, though he deploys it in the context of an overwrought analysis of all-consuming love and fatal heartbreak. By his account, an early death is a kind of mercy, a gift of God, sparing the victim many other "deaths": the loss of friends, lovers, youth, and everything else except breathing. So an "early grave" is not really cause for weeping; it "may be meant to save" us from the inevitable pains and disappointments of age.

Byron's rendition of this Greek idea is the one we remember, but there had been earlier attempts. The obscure 16th-century Englishman William Hugh had the first go at it, producing the clunky "most happy are they, and best beloved of God, that die when they are young." A few years later the rhetorician Thomas Wilson tried the more concise but ultimately forgettable "Whom God loveth best, those he taketh soonest." Poet George Herbert tried a negative version: "Those that God loves do not live long." The fourth time was the charm.

Truth Is Stranger Than Fiction

'T is strange,—but true; for Truth is always
    strange—
  Stranger than fiction: if it could be told,
How much would novels gain by the exchange!
  How differently the World would men behold!
How oft would Vice and Virtue places change!
  The new world would be nothing to the old,
If some Columbus of the moral seas
Would show mankind their Souls' antipodes.

Byron, *Don Juan,* Canto XIV, stanza ci

∽⚬∾

As he often does in what he called his "Epic Satire," Byron puts the action on hold to deliver a small sermon on man's hypocrisy. The occasion this time is his recollection, in the middle of describing one of Don Juan's sexual exploits, of an exploit of his own. We're not given the whole story, but we do know that it has something to do with a "harmless game at billiards." (Literary scholars, attentive to such details, have tracked down a letter describing the liaison, which involved a certain Lady Frances Webster.)

Anyway, the point to all this is that the whole billiard game episode, strange enough in itself, led to even stranger consequences (bringing Byron "to the brink / Of ruin"), which all goes to show how strange life can be. And "Truth is always strange," Byron quips—"Stranger than fiction."

Real life *is* often more surprising and weird than novels, but Byron takes this observation a step further. Its not that novelists are incapable of describing real events— plenty of them have. It's that they usually wind up couching their descriptions in entertaining or pleasant fictions, rather than going for the startling truth.

In other words, they fall back on the generally accepted ideas, judgments, and morality, playing to the sensibilities of their audience. But to Byron this is a cop-out, a refusal to tell it like it is. If more writers faced the truth and reported it unflinchingly, we might see that what we call Virtue is often Vice, and (vice versa) Vice, Virtue. What we need, Byron says, is a "Columbus of the moral seas" to discover the real terrain of the human soul. (*Antipodes* means the underside or opposing pole, literally the spot on the globe directly opposite where we are.)

Beauty Is Truth, Truth Beauty

O Attic shape! Fair attitude! with brede
  Of marble men and maidens overwrought,
With forest branches and the trodden weed;
  Thou, silent form, dost tease us out of thought
As doth eternity; Cold Pastoral!
  When old age shall this generation waste,
    Thou shalt remain, in midst of other woe
  Than ours, a friend to man, to whom thou
    say'st,
Beauty is truth, truth beauty,—that is all
  Ye know on earth, and all ye need to know.

John Keats, "Ode on a Grecian Urn" (1819),
41–50

"Beauty is truth, truth beauty" is the most famous line ever spoken by a pot, the "Grecian urn" of this poem's title. It's too bad the urn doesn't explain what it means; it would have spared posterity a lot of confusion.

If ever a poet were attuned to the ravages of time, it was John Keats (1795–1821). Stricken at age 21 by a congenital tubercular disease, he composed against time, needing to say everything he knew, knowing his time was short. He died at 25, already one of the greatest of all English poets.

His "Ode on a Grecian Urn"—his best work save for "Ode to a Nightingale"—is a lovely, heartbreaking meditation on time and loss. The poem's speaker regards an ancient Greek ceremonial pot adorned with sylvan scenes of music, repose, and lusty pursuit. A piper, frozen in art, plays a silent song, whose timeless music comes alive in the speaker's imagination. Unlike mortal things, this song is "forever new" (line 24). Likewise, the urn's lovers are "Forever panting, and forever young" (27), suspended in perpetual desire, never to experience loss or pain.

This pastoral scene, untouched by time, promises a kind of eternal youth: Life is short, but art is long. So long as the urn touches each viewer's imagination—the way Keats's lines touch the reader's—it will come alive anew. But at the same time the urn and its figures, mute and frigid, are dead things, deader than the culture that produced them because never alive to begin with.

Thus the "Cold Pastoral" of Keats's last verse, frozen in its "attitude," *overwrought* (covered over, but also overdone) with a *brede* (highly artificial pattern) of "marble men and maidens." Yes, it is beautiful, but what is the "truth" it seems to utter in the speaker's mind?

This is just one of many unanswered questions raised by the last two lines, whose mysteries make the poem perfect fodder for college English exams. Another uncertainty: Does the urn speak just the "Beauty is truth, truth beauty" part, or the remainder of the poem too? And more: If the speaker believes that the urn is an eternal "friend to man," does Keats?

Practically every critic answers these questions differently—at least, the critics who don't simply throw up their hands. Perhaps the simplest interpretation is the truest: Namely, that by lifting us out of everyday experiences and pains, beautiful objects bring us to contemplate more eternal realities and truths. Agree or disagree in an essay of 500 words.

The Later 19th Century

While in England the post-Romantic period brought a cooling off of poetic intensity, things were just warming up in the States. America's prose was better than its poetry—vastly better; but even the mediocre verse of Poe, Emerson, and Longfellow was a giant step from the yawning gulf that preceded it. Those poets prepared the way for the giants—Walt Whitman and Emily Dickinson—who in their distinct ways set a course for the future.

Meanwhile, across the Atlantic, Queen Victoria began her long and prosperous imperial reign, ushering in an age of conservative retrenchment. Thanks mostly to the Industrial Revolution, Britain's middle class prospered— though at terrible expense to the poor—and its cultural values triumphed. As the middle class grew, so did the market for literature, especially sentimental and nostalgic literature that offered escape from the more disturbing effects of progress (poverty, industrial blight, threatening new evolutionary theories, etc.).

But English taste was hardly uniform, and reactions to the times—in prose, poetry, science, religion, and politics—diverse. No one movement or philosophy comprises Victorian poetry; no one label—not "post-Romantic" or "pre-Raphaelite" or even "Victorian"—properly defines it. There's practically no way to get Tennyson, the Brownings, and Carroll into one sentence, except trivially. With the Americans mixed in, the picture looks even more incoherent. On the other hand, sometimes it's a relief to be rid of categories.

In this hodgepodge of a chapter, I cite poems by the following authors:

Edgar Allan Poe (1809–1849): an orphan from Boston, Poe aspired to poetry but hacked out prose for a living; called the inventor of the short story, the detective story, the horror tale, and other genres; his greatest success was in France, thanks to Baudelaire's translations;

Ralph Waldo Emerson (1803–1882): a Harvard man and minister who quit the clergy to pursue his Transcendental philosophy of mind and nature (whereby nature is thought in concrete form); celebrated today for his essays and lectures, which were far more influential than his poetry;

Henry Wadsworth Longfellow (1807–1882): the first white man to try writing like a Native; a professor of languages at Harvard and a great traveler; a prolific and popular poet in his time, now very out of fashion;

Alfred, Lord Tennyson (1809–1892): the dominant English poet of the period, though his reputation since has had its downs; a melancholic master of poetic music whose big themes are loss and doubt; successor to Wordsworth as poet laureate;

Elizabeth Barrett Browning (1806–1861): a great lyric love poet whose sonnets have remained popular for over a century; lived mostly in Italy with her husband, Robert; unconventional author of the ambitious blank-verse "novel" *Aurora Leigh*;

Robert Browning (1812–1889): husband of Elizabeth Barrett; though Tennyson was more highly esteemed, Browning was lots more interesting; wrote a new type of poetic monologue in which the poet disappears and the speaker unravels his own psyche;

WALT WHITMAN (1819–1892): world-class American egotist who wrote thousands of lines about himself; simultaneously a great humanitarian who cared for the wounded during the Civil War; boldly proclaimed that he would invent a truly American poetry and then did so;

EMILY DICKINSON (1830–1886): an agoraphobic recluse in Amherst, Massachusetts; wrote more than 1,000 poems, only two of which were published in her lifetime; severely religious and acutely sensitive; shunned punctuation marks; her reputation today is stratospheric;

LEWIS CARROLL (1832–1898): pen name of Charles Lutwidge Dodgson, Oxford math professor and amateur photographer; brilliant logician, punster, and satirist; wrote *Alice's Adventures in Wonderland* and *Through the Looking Glass* for Alice Liddell, one of his favorite photographic subjects; creator of the Cheshire Cat, Humpty Dumpty, the Mad Hatter, the White Rabbit, Tweedledum, Tweedledee, and other beloved characters;

GERARD MANLEY HOPKINS (1844–1889): English Jesuit priest and professor of Greek at Dublin University; experimented with rhythmic patterns and neologisms; unpublished in his lifetime but later warmly embraced by modern poets, who admired his technical innovations;

GELETT BURGESS (1866–1951): never saw a purple cow; regretted that he ever said so;

OSCAR WILDE (1854–1900): believed that the proper aim of art is "the telling of beautiful untrue things"; believed also that this is the proper aim of life; the greatest wit of his century, and one of the great comic dramatists in English; his best poems, "De Profundis" and "The Ballad of Reading Gaol," were written in prison, where he spent two years after being convicted of sodomy.

Other famous poets of the period include Matthew Arnold, Edward Lear, Algernon Charles Swinburne, and Thomas Hardy.

The Glory That Was Greece, and the Grandeur That Was Rome

> On desperate seas long wont to roam,
>   Thy hyacinth hair, thy classic face,
> Thy Naiad airs have brought me home
>   To the glory that was Greece
>   And the grandeur that was Rome.

Edgar Allan Poe, "To Helen" (1831), 6–10

Poe is celebrated now as a writer of horror and detective stories, but he wrote them mostly for the money. He really wanted to be a poet, and he published three books of poems before ever writing fiction. This poem, from his third collection, is the best of these early works. Poe claimed that he wrote the first draft when he was 14, in honor of a young lady who died a year later. The poem, which is kind of a muddle, is more or less an exercise in the English Romantic style.

Helen was not the young lady's name (it was Jane); she's reborn here as the legendary Greek beauty whose rape by a Trojan prince launched a thousand ships. But the real subject is greater even than the Greek Helen; her "classic face" stands in for the whole of Classical culture—the glory of Greece, the grandeur of Rome. Her "Naiad airs" (water-nymph songs) are echoes of a distant world, frozen in time like the figures on Keats's Grecian urn (page 167)—beautiful partly *because* they're dead.

The grammar of this stanza might lead you to think that it's Helen (or Helen's hyacinth hair) that roams the desperate seas. But the despair is Poe's; Helen, along with other classical figures such as Odysseus and Psyche, serves as a calming ideal of beauty, tranquility, and perfection. The irony, which (knowing Poe) might be intentional, is that the Greek beauty was far from a calming influence in her day. Behind the ideals of Greece and Rome lay the ruins of Troy, Carthage, and many another civilization.

Quoth the Raven, "Nevermore"

> Once upon a midnight dreary, while I pondered,
>   weak and weary,
> Over many a quaint and curious volume of for-
>   gotten lore—
> While I nodded, nearly napping, suddenly there
>   came a tapping,
> As of some one gently rapping, rapping at my
>   chamber door.
> "'T is some visitor," I muttered, "tapping at my
>   chamber door—
>   Only this and nothing more."…
>
> Open here I flung the shutter, when, with many a
>   flirt and flutter

In there stepped a stately Raven of the saintly
    days of yore.
Not the least obeisance made he; not a minute
    stopped or stayed he;
But, with mien of lord or lady, perched above my
    chamber door—
Perched upon a bust of Pallas just above my
    chamber door—
        Perched, and sat, and nothing more.

Then this ebony bird beguiling my sad fancy into
    smiling,
By the grave and stern decorum of the counte-
    nance it wore,
"Though thy crest be shorn and shaven, thou," I
    said, "art sure no craven,
Ghastly grim and ancient Raven wandering from
    the Nightly shore—
Tell me what thy lordly name is on the Night's
    Plutonian shore!"
        Quoth the Raven, "Nevermore."

    Poe, "The Raven" (1845), 1–6, 31–42

For all its mystery and psychological intensity, this, the most famous American poem of the 19th century, was written with an almost clinical attention to a set of pseudoscientific rules. If we are to believe what Poe himself wrote in his essay "The Philosophy of Composition" (1846), he set out with "The Raven" to write a poem of the ideal length (about 100 lines) producing the proper poetic result (Beauty) with the most suitable emotional tone (Melancholy), calculated to appeal both to critics and to the public. So much for what he called the "fine frenzy" and "ecstatic intuition" to which many poets chalk up their poems.

The poem's chilling refrain—"Nevermore"—was also deliberately calculated. Its melancholic monotony, repeated stanza after stanza, becomes a kind of hammer-blow on the speaker's mind. What does it mean? The Raven—a bird of ill omen—certainly can't say, so the meaning must be deduced by the increasingly deranged narrator. And why is the narrator—a student—susceptible to derangement? Because his imagination is overactive, but more so because his lover Lenore has recently died. (Quoth Poe: "The death...of a beautiful woman is, unquestionably, the most poetical topic in the world.")

The bereaved lover *knows* the bird is just mindlessly parroting the word "Nevermore," but at the same time he's led by superstition and melancholy to take the Raven's refrain as significant. In fact, he begins shaping his questions in expectation of the refrain. (Poe alludes to the "human thirst for self-torture.") His first query is harmless: He asks the bird its name. Obviously, the Raven's reply makes little sense; but it seems more apt as the speaker continues. He urges himself to forget Lenore; the bird says "Nevermore." He wonders whether his grief will ever be soothed; the bird says, "Nevermore." Will he meet his love in the afterlife? "Nevermore." He screams at the bird to "take thy beak from out my heart"; the Raven answers, "Nevermore."

And in fact the bird never leaves; it sits still on that bust of Pallas (Greek goddess of wisdom), casting its evil shadow on the speaker's floor. And the speaker sinks into a hopeless state of dark despair, his soul trapped in the shadow, "nevermore" to be rescued. He's become a kind of parrot himself, repeating that melancholy word, pounding himself down deeper into despair. By the end, the Raven becomes unnecessary, for the student has internalized it. It has become, in Poe's words, merely an emblem of "Mournful and Never-ending Remembrance."

The Shot Heard Round the World

By the rude bridge that arched the flood,
    Their flag to April's breeze unfurled,
Here once the embattled farmers stood,
    And fired the shot heard round the world.

Ralph Waldo Emerson, "Hymn: Sung at the
Completion of the Concord Monument"
(1836), 1–4

Ralph Waldo Emerson, the American philosopher and Unitarian minister best known for such essays as "Self-Reliance" and "Experience," wasn't often given to patriotic cheerleading. But his soul was stirred by the erection of a monument to the Revolutionary minutemen in his hometown of Concord. The result was this unfortunate hymn, which was to be sung at the monument's dedication on April 19, 1836, the 61st anniversary of the battles of Lexington and Concord.

In case your American history is rusty, these two battles marked the official beginning of the Revolutionary War. The British, alarmed at the colonists' growing stockpiles of weapons, marched on Lexington to begin seizing them. They were met there by a hastily assembled militia, called "minutemen," who only briefly detained them.

Then it was on to Concord, where the Redcoats met stiffer resistance at a "rude bridge" over the Concord River. Here the minutemen managed to turn the King's men back with a volley of ammo, which Emerson collectively dubs the "shot heard round the world." What he means is that the colonists' resistance sent a loud signal to the courts and capitals of Europe (France in particular) that a new era had begun, and that tyranny and injustice would be resisted. If the shot was heard in Africa or Asia, I doubt anyone cared very much.

Emerson claims that the shot was fired by farmers, but the historical record shows this is mostly untrue. According to Richard Shenkman's *Legends, Lies, and Cherished Myths of American History,* the average minuteman was "poor, landless, out of work, and out of hope." Many a farmer chose to sit the battle out, paying some desperate soul to do his fighting for him. Most of the minutemen couldn't shoot straight, either, and history would probably have taken a very different turn if they didn't outnumber the British by about two to one.

ॐ

Into Each Life Some Rain Must Fall

Be still, sad heart! and cease repining;
Behind the clouds is the sun still shining;
Thy fate is the common fate of all,
Into each life some rain must fall,
    Some days must be dark and dreary.

Henry Wadsworth Longfellow,
"The Rainy Day" (1841), 11–15

Even happy people get sad, and even smart people write bad poetry. Longfellow, a professor of modern languages first at Bowdoin and then at Harvard, wrote some of the very worst poetry known to man. On the other hand, his verse is bad in a simple, straightforward, and sentimental way, which made it popular then and almost forgivable now.

What's hard to forgive is the easy smugness of someone who tells you that "Into each life some rain must fall." When in pain, one is not likely to appreciate so banal and generic a comfort, however much it worked for Longfellow. The weather metaphor only makes things worse, because weather is the classic refuge of people who have nothing else to say.

At least in Longfellow's case he's talking to himself. In the first stanza he complains that the day is "cold, dark, and dreary," rainy and gloomy, windy and miserable. In the second stanza we discover that his life, too, is cold, dark, and dreary, metaphorically rainy, gloomy, windy, and miserable. Then comes the redemptive third stanza, quoted here, in which Longfellow suddenly realizes that sometimes life is tough, that sometimes we feel sad, and that, like the weather, our moods come and go.

One If by Land, Two If by Sea

Listen, my children, and you shall hear
Of the midnight ride of Paul Revere,
On the eighteenth of April, in Seventy-five;
Hardly a man is now alive
Who remembers that famous day and year.

He said to his friend, "If the British march
By land or sea from the town to-night,
Hang a lantern aloft in the belfry arch
Of the North Church tower as a signal light,—
One, if by land, and two, if by sea;
And I on the opposite shore will be,
Ready to ride and spread the alarm
Through every Middlesex village and farm,
For the country folk to be up and to arm."

Longfellow, *Tales of a Wayside Inn*, Part I
(1863), *Paul Revere's Ride*, 1–14

The midnight ride of Paul Revere in April 1775 is one of the most famous events in American history. So you may be surpised to learn that at the time nobody thought it was a very big deal. Revere, a Boston silversmith, was seen as a minor, if helpful, figure, and then he was practically forgotten. It was Longfellow, 88 years later, who made Revere a national hero, and who coined the line "One if by land, two if by sea."

Longfellow enhanced the tale in other ways, too. In his poem, Revere is a lone rider who brings the minutemen word that the British are coming by sea. But in real life Revere was one of three riders, and he never finished the job. After warning the Lexington minutemen, who

would fail their assignment (page 177), Revere was captured by the British, so he never made it to Concord.

Longfellow embroidered the truth for rhetorical
effect, which was certainly nothing new, and certainly
nothing to blame. (Shakespeare, for one, did exactly the
same in his history plays.) What's interesting is that the
poem has so utterly trumped the historical record; Revere's
fictional ride is far more famous than the actual facts.

Ships That Pass in the Night

> Ships that pass in the night, and speak each other
> in passing,
> Only a signal shown and distant voice in the
> darkness;
> So on the ocean of life, we pass and speak one
> another,
> Only a look and a voice, then darkness again and
> silence.

> Longfellow, *Tales of a Wayside Inn,* Part III
> (1873), *The Theologian's Tale,* iv, 1–4

Longfellow's *Tales of a Wayside Inn,* like the *Canterbury
Tales,* is a story about people telling stories. The setting is
the cozy Red-Horse Inn in Sudbury, Massachusetts, about
20 miles from Cambridge, where Longfellow taught. A
group of anonymous friends—identified only by nation-
ality or profession—gather around the fireplace to enter-
tain each other with diverting tales, both historical and
legendary. The book, first published in parts and then

united in 1874, is padded out with various "interludes" reminiscent of Chaucer's prologues.

In his third turn, the Theologian tells the tale of Elizabeth Haddon, a recent immigrant from England who has settled on a farm near the Delaware River. Elizabeth is a very, very godly soul who speaks hardly a sentence without praising the Lord, and who does nothing without His guidance. In particular, when she falls in love she does so under God's direction. But when she reveals the Lord's will to the lucky guy, he regrets to say that he has business to attend to, also per the Lord's instructions. He sails off the next day and that, for the moment, is that.

So it goes for us all on the ocean of life, says Longfellow. We are like "ships that pass in the night," tooting out our little signals to one another before moving on into the solitary darkness. Except, as the story goes on to prove, it isn't always like that. Patient Elizabeth continues to lead a saint's life, and eventually her man is steered back her way. God joins them up, starboard to port, and they sail off together in holy matrimony.

'Tis Better to Have Loved and Lost Than Never to Have Loved at All

I envy not in any moods
   The captive void of noble rage,
   The linnet born within the cage,
That never knew the summer woods;

I envy not the beast that takes
   His license in the field of time,

Unfettered by the sense of crime,
To whom a conscience never wakes;

Nor, what may count itself as blest,
  The heart that never plighted troth
  But stagnates in the weeds of sloth;
Nor any want-begotten rest.

I hold it true, whate'er befall;
  I feel it, when I sorrow most;
  'Tis better to have loved and lost
Than never to have loved at all.

Alfred, Lord Tennyson, *In Memoriam A. H. H.*
(1850), section 27

The product of 17 years' labor, *In Memoriam A. H. H.* is a lengthy and diverse collection of meditations on loss. Its initial inspiration was the death of the poet's best friend, Arthur H. Hallam, in 1833, but Tennyson kept adding material until its publication in 1850, the year he was named England's poet laureate.

Several of the poem's 127 sections (plus prologue and epilogue) grapple with one question: What's the good of caring about anything when caring only exposes us to loss and pain? The answer: Pain is the necessary prelude to spiritual growth. The man who has no care, though secure from grief, is no better than a "beast" without conscience.

Thus Tennyson's most famous lines, "'Tis better to have loved and lost / Than never to have loved at all." *Love* means any deep attachment, not just sexual love—the case in point is his friendship with Hallam. Nonetheless, the lines have become in time trite comfort to heartsick adolescents, a fate anticipated in Tennyson's lifetime, even before the finished poem was published. The poet

Thomas Campbell, who parodied other famous contemporaries, wrote in 1842 that it is "Better to be courted and jilted / Than never be courted at all." Later, in the posthumous *Way of All Flesh* (1903), Samuel Butler took another parodic crack: "'Tis better to have loved and lost, than never to have lost at all."

Ring Out the Old, Ring In the New

Ring out, wild bells, to the wild sky,
   The flying cloud, the frosty light:
   The year is dying in the night:
Ring out, wild bells, and let him die.

Ring out the old, ring in the new,
   Ring, happy bells, across the snow:
   The year is going, let him go;
Ring out the false, ring in the true.

Ring out the grief that saps the mind,
   For those that here we see no more;
   Ring out the feud of rich and poor,
Ring in redress to all mankind.

Tennyson, *In Memoriam A. H. H.,* section 106

We think of the opening line as a New Year's chant, but the bells Tennyson hears are Christmas bells. A week hardly matters, though, when one is so eager to be rid of the year.

Markings of time are good for the psyche. Although time may steal away all things, including loved ones, it renews itself at the turning of the year. In this section

Tennyson depicts not a foolish optimism—he could hardly have believed that in one year rich and poor would make friends—but rather, the heart's resilience, its ability to hope for better in proportion to its pain, despite the harshness of reality. The verses are an invocation, not a prediction.

In recent years Tennyson's verses were revived in the lyrics of George Harrison's "Ding Dong, Ding Dong."

After Many a Summer Dies the Swan

> The woods decay, the woods decay and fall,
> The vapors weep their burthen to the ground,
> Man comes and tills the field and lies beneath,
> And after many a summer dies the swan.
> Me only cruel immortality
> Consumes; I wither slowly in thine arms,
> Here at the quiet limit of the world....
>
> Tennyson, "Tithonius" (1833–1860), 1–7

This poem, which lent a title to yet another of Aldous Huxley's novels, beautifies the Greek myth of Tithonius. According to the legend, Eos, goddess of dawn, fell in love with Tithonius, brother of King Priam of Troy. Eos begs Zeus to make Tithonius immortal, and the top god complies. Unfortunately, Eos forgot to ask for eternal youth on the side.

⁓

As a result, Tithonius is condemned to age eternally, and after a while there's barely anything left of him. In Tennyson's words, he's merely a "gray shadow, once a man." As the poem begins, Tithonius laments that he cannot die as everything else: Trees are allowed to die, clouds (*vapors*) are allowed to die, other men are allowed to die, and "after many a summer dies the swan." Only Tithonius is condemned to decay without end.

Tithonius may choose the swan as his animal example because swans, in Greek legend, die a particularly beautiful death. Realizing their time is near, they warble out a haunting cry, immortalized in the annals of cliché as their "swan song." If it's any consolation, Tithonius's song is also beautiful, one of Tennyson's best, written while the poet himself was gripped by a death wish. (His best friend A. H. Hallam had recently passed his last summer—see page 182.)

What happens to Tithonius next varies among the Greek versions of his tale. In some he continues to shrivel away until, like the nymph Echo, all that remains is his voice. In other accounts, the gods have pity and transform him to a grasshopper—the insect with a big voice and a slight body.

Theirs Is Not to Reason Why

"Forward, the Light Brigade!"
Was there a man dismayed?
Not though the soldier knew
Someone had blundered.
Theirs not to make reply,

Theirs not to reason why,
Theirs but to do and die.
Into the valley of Death
  Rode the six hundred.

> Tennyson, "The Charge of the Light
> Brigade" (1854), 9–17

On the occasion of a famously doomed military maneuver, Tennyson wrote a famously bad piece. A so-called "newspaper poem," he dashed it off in the belief that, as England's poet laureate, he should versify national tragedies. At the time many found it stirring, and its title would become a memorable phrase; also famous are the lines "Theirs not to reason why, / Theirs but to do and die." The rest is best forgotten.

The event in question occurred during the Crimean War of 1853–56, in which England, France, and Turkey were allied against Russia. The Russians had seized various Turkish outposts on the coast of Crimea, and then attacked England's Heavy Brigade (artillerymen) stationed in the area.

The English botched their response. A series of miscommunications resulted in the dispatch of the Light Brigade—cavalrymen armed only with sabers—to confront the enemy at Balaclava, a port town near Sebastopol. Six hundred horsemen went up against thousands of Russians, and roughly 450 Englishmen died before the rest retreated.

Tennyson's poem celebrates the heroism of soldiers who follow orders, no matter how stupid—"Theirs not to reason why." His heavily rhymed, four-beat lines don't allow for much in the way of subtle thought, but Tennyson intended to write a public ballad, not an introspective lyric.

How Do I Love Thee? Let Me Count the Ways

How do I love thee? Let me count the ways.
I love thee to the depth and breadth and height
My soul can reach, when feeling out of sight
For the ends of Being and ideal Grace.
I love thee to the level of everyday's
Most quiet need, by sun and candle light.
I love thee freely, as men strive for Right;
I love thee purely, as they turn from Praise.
I love thee with the passion put to use
In my old griefs, and with my childhood's faith.
I love thee with a love I seemed to lose
With my lost saints—I love thee with the breath,
Smiles, tears, of all my life!—and, if God choose,
I shall but love thee better after death.

Elizabeth Barrett Browning, *Sonnets from the
Portuguese* (1850), Sonnet 43

Those who quote this most trite of all poetic love tributes don't often stop to consider what it says. (Rule One: The more clichéd the phrase, the less important its literal meaning.) They mean something like "I love you in more ways than I can count"; but Barrett Browning counts, and the total is eight (allowing for God).

It's too bad for Barrett Browning that she's best remembered for coining a corny line; she was actually an excellent lyric poet, more popular while she lived than her now more esteemed husband Robert Browning. This sonnet, for example, is a lovely tribute to their mutual devotion, even though she shifts feet in the last two lines.

You might think, from the title of Barrett Browning's sonnet collection, that she stole the whole thing from a Portuguese original. But she wrote them all from scratch—the Portuguese thing appears to be an inside joke.

God's in His Heaven—All's Right with the World

The year's at the spring
And day's at the morn;
Morning's at seven;
The hill-side's dew-pearled;
The lark's on the wing;
The snail's on the thorn:
God's in his heaven—
All's right with the world!

Robert Browning, *Pippa Passes* (1841),
Part I, 221–28

"God's in his heaven—all's right with the world": a final-ist in the Most Misquoted Phrase contest. In many cases, Browning's exact attitude is elusive, so you can quote his lines in most any context you please. This is not such a case.

Browning was a master of subtle, deadpan irony, but the irony here is blunt. Pippa, a young girl who works in an Italian silk mill, is singing a song outside a house on the morning of New Year's Day. Thus the year's not "at spring," nor, as it happens, is it seven o'clock.

In fact, nothing in the song is true; even if God's in his heaven, all is definitely *not* right with the world. For inside the house are Ottima and her lover, Sebald, co-conspirators in the recent murder of Ottima's husband. They're in the middle of a dreadful scene when they overhear Pippa's song, which couldn't contrast more starkly with what's going on inside.

If you've ever used Pippa's line in earnest, there's some consolation. Pippa herself isn't fully aware of the irony of the situation. And it's unlikely anybody knew you were quoting out of context—*Pippa Passes,* a collection of "dramatic scenes," has barely been read in recent memory.

It All Comes to the Same Thing at the End

Re-coin thyself and give it them to spend,—
It all comes to the same thing at the end,
  Since mine thou wast, mine art and mine shalt
    be,
Faithful or faithless, sealing up the sum
Or lavish of my treasure, thou must come
  Back to the heart's place here I keep for thee!

Robert Browning, "Any Wife to
Any Husband" (1854), 91–96

In this poetic monologue, a dying wife reflects on her husband's obvious devotion and, she fears, its limits. She has nothing to complain of yet: He's been the model of the loving spouse. But she knows human nature, and knows that all things fade.

Like "any wife," she hopes he will never remarry; she uses the poem, in fact, to try arguing him out of it, though the thought may never have crossed his mind. He might tell himself, she says, that no new love can erase the love he had for her, which they'll find again in the hereafter. He might think that whether he marries again or not, "It all comes to the same thing at [not *in*] the end" (meaning doomsday).

Though the wife coins this phrase, she doesn't mean a word of it. Is it so hard, she asks, for her husband to live out what's left of his life without straying from her "heart's place"? "Why should it be with stain at all?" she demands, adding that if their places were changed, she'd show him the real meaning of constant, true love. (Of course, he'd be dead, but she thinks the dead keep an eye on the living.)

The wife's desire is quite understandable, but she protests too much, winding up rather unsympathetic. Nonetheless, Browning had more sympathy for his poetic wife's argument than his real wife did. Elizabeth Barrett Browning—who wasn't just any wife—actively *encouraged* Robert to remarry should he outlive her. (He did outlive her, and stayed single.) In the poem, a wife criticizes her husband for something he seems to have no intention of doing; in real life, a wife criticizes her husband for vowing *not* to remarry. No matter what, a guy can't win.

His Reach Exceeds His Grasp
and Less Is More

I do what many dream of, all their lives,
—Dream? strive to do, and agonize to do,
And fail in doing. I could count twenty such
On twice your fingers, and not leave this town,
Who strive—you don't know how the others
    strive
To paint a little thing like that you smeared
Carelessly passing with your robes afloat—
Yet do so much less, so much less, Someone says
(I know his name, no matter)—so much less!
Well, less is more, Lucrezia: I am judged....
Ah, but a man's reach should exceed his grasp,
Or what's a heaven for? All is silver-gray
Placid and perfect with my art: the worse!
I know both what I want and what might gain,
An yet how profitless to know, to sigh
"Had I been two, another and myself,
Our head would have o'erlooked the world!" No
    doubt.

       Robert Browning, "Andrea del Sarto"
         (1855), 69–78, 97–103

This poem begins in the middle of a domestic argument between sixteenth-century Florentine painter Andrea del Sarto and his wife, Lucrezia. But we only hear del Sarto's voice, a 277-line dramatic monologue, with no reply from Lucrezia nor any interruption by the author.

    This sort of poem—one long seamless quotation—was more or less Browning's invention, though he obviously drew on the theater. (He'd earlier tried his hand at drama but failed.) No poet since has equaled Browning's mastery of the form, in which characters reveal themselves only through what they say, though they always reveal more than they intend.

The topic of del Sarto's monologue isn't marital friction, but his own curious lack of greatness. Known as "the Faultless Painter" for his impeccable technique, del Sarto nonetheless painted no masterpiece—he just didn't have the drive. His explanation here is a paradox: He's less than great because he's so good. Since he doesn't have to struggle to produce perfect paintings, he has slipped into complacency—all is placid and perfect, the worse for his art.

So when he exclaims "Ah, but a man's reach should exceed his grasp," he's actually wishing that it did—contrary to how we usually use his line today. If his did, he'd have to strive after the *heaven* of perfection. For what's the use of heaven—that is, humanly unattainable perfection—if not to inspire us to strive for it?

But del Sarto doesn't struggle or strive like his less facile peers, such as Michelangelo (the "Someone" in line 76). They labor more and achieve less; but as he says, "less is more": their work is imperfect in execution but heavenly in effect.

Though Browning coined this latter phrase, he rarely gets the credit for it. Rather, the honors usually go to German architect Ludwig Mies van der Rohe (1886–1969), who heard it from his teacher Peter Behrens, who found it kicking around the German art world in the earlier 20th century.

I Sing the Body Electric

I sing the body electric,
The armies of those I love engirth me and I
    engirth them,
They will not let me off till I go with them,
    respond to them,
And discorrupt them, and charge them full with
    the charge of the soul.

Was it doubted that those who corrupt their own
    bodies conceal themselves?
And if those who defile the living are as bad as
    they who defile the dead?
And if the body does not do fully as much as the
    soul?
And if the body were not the soul, what is the
    soul?

Walt Whitman, "I Sing the Body Electric"
(1855), 1–8

One of the few great American poets before this century, Walt Whitman was also one of the first to write free verse. His lines tumble on without regard to length or meter; and though he often repeats line endings, he practically never really rhymes. In this, as in his fierce assertion that body and soul are one, he has a predecessor in Blake, and a successor in Allen Ginsberg.

"I Sing the Body Electric" was one of twelve sprawling poems in the original, anonymous 1855 edition of *Leaves of Grass,* which grew over the years to ultimately include 389 poems in a final 1892 edition. The phrase "I sing" is a chant often repeated through the work in its various editions; "I celebrate myself, and sing myself" was its original, defiantly individualistic first line. Whitman saw himself as the very embodiment of the American spirit, so that by singing himself he was singing America.

In this poem he sings a more general song, applicable to all mankind though most fully realized in the people of his vibrant, free-spirited nation. He sings to celebrate the body, but not simply as a physical thing; he sings the "body electric," the body as embodiment and vehicle of the soul's energy or "charge." Like Blake (page 153), he views his poetic mission as burning off the dead layers of shame and corruption layered on the body by ages of moralistic repression.

Needless to say, this approach didn't earn him the gratitude of the nation he thought he was celebrating. Though a popular flop, he did have his fans, including writers such as Ralph Waldo Emerson and Oscar Wilde. In the 20th century he would find a wider readership, and would greatly influence writers such as William Carlos Williams and the American Beat poets.

When Lilacs Last in the Dooryard Bloomed...

> When lilacs last in the dooryard bloom'd,
> And the great star early droop'd in the western
>   sky in the night,
> I mourn'd, and yet shall mourn with ever-return-
>   ing spring.
>
> Ever-returning spring, trinity sure to me you
>   bring,
> Lilac blooming perennial and drooping star in the
>   west,
> And thought of him I love.
>
>   Whitman, "When Lilacs Last in the
>   Dooryard Bloom'd" (1865), 1–6

This is a poem about memory, the first in a series Whitman called "Memories of President Lincoln." It is a recollection of the night of April 14, 1865, when John Wilkes Booth shot Lincoln at Ford's Theater in Washington.

Shocking or sad news tends to heighten our senses, sharpening our perceptions of the things around us; these things then become constant reminders, transporting us back to that scene. "I remember where I was stopping at the time," Whitman later said;

> the season being advanced, there were many lilacs
> in full bloom. By one of those caprices that enter
> and give tinge to events without being at all a
> part of them, I find myself always reminded of the
> great tragedy of that day by the sight and odor of
> those blossoms.

Lilacs were very popular in Whitman's America, fragrantly blooming each spring in many a *dooryard* (front yard). Their beauty is almost cruelly discordant with the memories they revive, and will revive, Whitman is sure, with each returning spring.

Also conjoined with the blooming lilacs is the "great star early droop'd in the western sky" in the night as Lincoln lay dying. The great star is actually the planet Venus, one of the brightest objects in the sky, which in April is set low in the west. Venus, great but "early droop'd," is clearly a symbol for the assassinated president, "him I love," whom Whitman heroized as the leading spirit of American democracy.

After Great Pain, a Formal Feeling Comes

> After great pain, a formal feeling comes—
> The Nerves sit ceremonious, like Tombs—
> The stiff Heart questions was it He, that bore,
> And Yesterday, or Centuries before?

> Emily Dickinson, poem no. 341 (1860s), 1–4

Along with Whitman, Emily Dickinson was one of the two great American poets of her century. But unlike Whitman, who refused to stop publishing, Dickinson hardly began. Hidden away in her lifelong Amherst home, she wrote a staggering number of poems—nearly 1,800—of which only a few were published in her lifetime.

Dickinson was the classic introvert, shy of human contact but possessed of a deep and dramatic inner life. Small events unleashed torrents of poetry, full of reflection and feeling though lacking in concrete detail. We can only guess at the "great pain" that inspired this poem, which may rarely be quoted but which is still one of her best-known.

Dickinson's subject is the numbness that sets in after we experience terrible pain. Her word is *formal,* meaning "stiff" but also "mechanical"—to the extent we continue to function, we're only going through the motions. Our heart, stunned, disconnects both from the pain and from the outer world that caused it; reality and time become confused. Was it really I that bore the pain, asks the heart, and was it yesterday or ages ago?

"This is the Hour of Lead," Dickinson writes; if we survive it, we remember it "As Freezing persons, recollect the Snow— / First—Chill—then Stupor—then the letting go—" (lines 12–13; the capitals and dashes are typical). The effects of pain are not overcome by resistance; we survive them only through surrender. A very religious woman, Dickinson may have been thinking of divine healing; either way, as we don't choose to feel pain, we can't choose to end it. We endure it, the chill withdraws, and we forget.

Beware the Jabberwock, My Son

> 'Twas brillig, and the slithy toves
> Did gyre and gimble in the wabe;
> All mimsy were the borogroves,
> And the mome raths outgrabe.

"Beware the Jabberwock, my son!
    The jaws that bite, the claws that catch!
Beware the Jubjub bird, and shun
    The frumious Bandersnatch!"

He took his vorpal sword in hand;
    Long time the manxome foe he sought—
So rested he by the Tumtum tree,
    And stood awhile in thought.

And, as in uffish thought he stood,
    The Jabberwock, with eyes of flame,
Came whiffling through the tulgey wood,
    And burbled as it came!

One, two! One, two! And through and through
    The vorpal blade went snicker-snack!
He left it dead, and with its head
    He went galumphing back.

"And hast thou slain the Jabberwock?
    Come to my arms, my beamish boy!
Oh frabjous day! Callooh! Callay!"
    He chortled in his joy.

'Twas brillig, and the slithy toves
    Did gyre and gimble in the wabe;
All mimsy were the borogroves,
    And the mome raths outgrabe.

Lewis Carroll, "Jabberwocky," from *Through
the Looking Glass* (1872)

Logician Charles Dodgson, better known as Lewis Carroll, always loved parodies and puns. In his youth he published the humorous newsletter *Misch-Masch* for the amusement of his siblings; the first verse of "Jabberwocky" appeared there in 1855. According to the author, it was an antique specimen of Anglo-Saxon poetry, and he proceeded to gloss the "archaic" terms. Here, courtesy of Martin Gardner's *Annotated Alice,* is what they mean:

• brillig: from *bryl* ("broil")—the "time of broiling dinner."

• slithy [pronounced *sly-thee*]: from *slimy* plus *lithe*—"smooth and active."

• tove: "A species of badger."

• gyre [hard g]: "To scratch like a dog" (from *gyaour* or *giaour,* "dog").

• gimble: "To screw out holes in anything."

• wabe: from *swab* ("soak")—"The side of a hill" (from its "being soaked in the rain").

• mimsy: "Unhappy" (same root as *miserable*).

• borogrove: "An extinct kind of Parrot. They had no wings, beaks turned up, and made their nests under sundials: lived on veal."

• mome: "Grave" (same root as *solemn*).

• rath: "A species of land turtle."

• outgrabe: "Squeaked" (past tense of *outgribe,* same root as *shriek*).

Now here's Carroll's "translation" into modern English:

> It was evening, and the smooth active badgers
> were scratching and boring holes in the hillside;
> all unhappy were the parrots; and the grave turtles
> squeaked out.

He goes on:

> There were probably sundials on the top of the
> hill, and the "borogroves" were afraid that their
> nests would be undermined. The hill was proba-
> bly full of the nests of "raths," which ran out,
> squeaking with fear, on hearing the "toves"
> scratching outside. This is an obscure, but yet
> deeply-affecting, relic of ancient Poetry.

This ridiculous series of notes is largely repeated, though occasionally modified, by Humpty Dumpty in *Through the Looking Glass.* ("And a 'borogrove,'" Humpty tells Alice, "is a thin shabby-looking bird with its feathers sticking out all round—something like a live mop.")

Unfortunately, Humpty stops there, and we have no interpreter for the poem's many other nonce-words. We're not even told what a "Jabberwock" is, though clearly it's some fearsome, dragonlike creature, of the ilk that stomped through ancient heroic ballads. The poem, which tests how we use context to make sense out of nonsense, is also a parody of these creaky old poems. And the biggest joke of all is that, despite his father's warning, it takes our hero fewer lines to dispatch the Jabberwock than it took to say "it was about dinner time."

Margaret, Are You Grieving…

Márgarét, are you gríeving
Over Goldengrove unleaving?
Leáves, líke the things of man, you
With your fresh thoughts care for, can you?
Áh! ás the heart grows older
It will come to such sights colder
By and by, nor spare a sigh
Though worlds of wanwood leafmeal lie;
And yet you wíll weep and know why.
Now no matter, child, the name:
Sow no matter, child, the name: Nor mouth had,
    no nor mind, expressed
What heart heard of, ghost guessed:
It is the blight man was born for,
It is Margaret you mourn for.

Gerard Manley Hopkins, "Spring and Fall"
(1880)

When first published in 1918, Hopkins's poems fit right in with the modern trends in poetry, though they'd actually been written four decades earlier. A devoted Jesuit, Hopkins refused to publish his work, which remained unknown at his death in 1889. His irregular rhythms and run-on verses, his linguistic experiments, and his highly compressed grammar, unique in Victorian poetry, went unappreciated by his contemporaries.

These qualities also make Hopkins hard to interpret. This, his most famous poem, begins on an easy, childlike note, but it doesn't stay that way for long. The speaker, who comes upon a child weeping at the end of spring (more like summer), means to introduce the little girl to very difficult and adult subjects.

The language follows suit. Some of Hopkins's touches are light, such as the pun *unleaving* in the second line. (The trees of Goldengrove—a generic nature spot—are losing their leaves, a fact playfully contradicted by the other meaning of *unleaving,* "refusing to leave.") Mostly, though, it's just hard to understand what's going on, despite the simple, Anglo-Saxon diction. For example, you'll probably have to read lines three and four—with their odd repeat rhyme and unexpected enjambment— several times before you can guess at their meaning. (Something like: "Can you really care that much about leaves, when the people around you are experiencing more painful losses? I suppose you can, since you're young and inexperienced.")

The gist of the poem is pretty dire. The speaker assures Margaret—who certainly didn't ask his advice—that if the falling of leaves seems bad now, there are going to be much worse things to cry about when she grows up. Little does she know how cold her future sorrows will be, and how little she'll care for the death of a season, though "worlds of wanwood leafmeal lie." (Hopkins invented both *wanwood,* perhaps meaning "pale trees," and *leafmeal,* "leaves having fallen piecemeal and crumbled." So far as I know, they were never used again.)

The remainder of the poem is full of allusions to a "fall" more saddening than the season—the Fall of Man. Though Margaret is too young to really grasp Original Sin (the "blight man was born for"), there's a knowledge of it in her heart and soul ("ghost"). And it, rather than the mere expiration of some leafmeal, is the true "spring" (another pun) of her sorrow. She grieves not for Golden-grove, but for her own inborn sinfulness.

The accent marks printed here were part of Hopkins's finished manuscript. He wanted to make sure you got the rhythm right, which requires deviating from the words' natural accentual pattern. Hopkins referred to the resulting clusters of stress as "sprung rhythm"—which adds another layer of punning to this poem's title.

I Never Saw a Purple Cow

> I never saw a purple cow,
> I never hope to see one;
> But I can tell you, anyhow,
> I'd rather see than be one.

Gelett Burgess, "The Purple Cow" (1895)

All that needs to be said about this poem—here quoted in its entirety—was said by the poet himself. In "Cinq Ans Après" (published in 1914, actually *dix-neuf ans après*), Burgess wrote:

> Ah, yes, I wrote the "Purple Cow"—
> I'm sorry, now, I wrote it!
> But I can tell you, anyhow,
> I'll kill you if you quote it.

Each Man Kills the Thing He Loves

Yet each man kills the thing he loves,
  By each let this be heard,
Some do it with a bitter look,
  Some with a flattering word,
The coward does it with a kiss,
  The brave man with a sword!

Some kill their love when they are young,
  And some when they are old;
Some strangle with the hands of Lust,
  Some with the hands of Gold;
The kindest use a knife, because
  The dead so soon grow cold.

Oscar Wilde, "The Ballad of Reading Gaol"
(1898), 37–48

Oscar Wilde was the wittiest writer since Alexander Pope, but he was also capable of amazing stupidity. In 1892, he became romantically involved with the Lord Alfred Douglas, much to the consternation of the latter's father, the Marquess of Queensberry. Queensberry publicly accused Wilde of sodomy; Wilde foolishly sued him for libel. The case was doomed from the start, and once Wilde got himself in court he never got out. In a second, criminal trial, he was found guilty of homosexual acts and slapped in Reading Gaol (or Jail, as the Americans spell it) for two years of hard labor.

Wilde's best writing till then—such as "The Decay of Lying" and *The Importance of Being Earnest*—had been lively satire, brazenly unserious. But in those days hard labor was very serious business, and out of his experience

Wilde produced a serious poem, "The Ballad of Reading Gaol."

The poem begins as he watches a condemned be led to the gallows for murdering his wife. Wilde, who had reason to question the concept of justice, wonders whether killing this man is truly just. Was his crime so great? Was it more horrible than the acts of respectable men who freely walk the streets?

The man is a murderer, it's true; but so are we all. For "each man kills the thing he loves"—only most do it with weapons other than knives. At least the condemned man's wife is out of her misery, in death "grown cold" to his hatred. The rest of us live to feel the hatred, the bitter words and heartless betrayals of those who once loved us. All of us have been there; none of us is guiltless.

Yet no one is hanged for cruelty. The man who makes his wife's life hell doesn't "die a death of shame / On a day of dark disgrace" (55–56). Wilde's not saying he should; he's giving us the other side of the picture. He shows us the emotional and physical torture he and his fellow prisoners undergo, for doing the same things the rest of us do by other means—with words rather than knives, with money rather than force. Wilde's moral equivalencies may not impress you, and few have ever shared his empathy for killers. Perhaps Wilde is just being shocking again. But morals have changed since his day, and at least we can sympathize with him.

William Butler Yeats

William Butler Yeats (1865–1939) was an odd bird, odd in the style of William Blake (page 148), his poetic progenitor and hero. Like Blake, he grappled with the age-old dualism of body and spirit, and like Blake he concocted his own bizarre symbolic system to explain their relation.

Unlike Blake, however, Yeats was recognized in his lifetime as a great poet, and he's now widely considered the greatest poet of the last hundred years. He initially planned to follow in his father's footsteps (and Blake's) as a painter, but after two years of art school he quit to write verse. He settled in Dublin, his birthplace, but traveled often to London and was engaged in both cities' literary circles. Politically, however, Yeats was a nationalist opposed to British control over Ireland. His nationalism was only strengthened when in 1889 he fell in love with Maud Gonne, an Irish firebrand, unrequiting lover, and major figure in Yeats's verse.

In poetry Yeats was influenced not only by Blake, but also by traditional Irish ballads, Romantic lyrics, and the writings of French *symbolistes* such as Baudelaire and Mallarmé (who in turn were inspired by Poe). Following the symbolists, he believed that material objects formed "correspondences" with immaterial objects and states, and that poetic symbols, properly arranged, could invoke a complex, otherwise ineffable spiritual reality. Yeats's poetry is full of such symbols, such as the rose, the cross, the tower, the moon, and his famous "gyres," which trace out historical and spiritual cycles. Symbolism would continue to have a profound, if less personal, effect on later poets such as Ezra Pound, T. S. Eliot, and Wallace Stevens.

Around the turn of the century, and after Maud Gonne had married another man, Yeats discovered two new enthusiasms, one for drama and the other for mystical occultism. In Dublin he established, managed, and wrote for a new theater, while dabbling in the "theosophy" of one Madame Blavatsky of New York, a philosophy Yeats eventually realized was baloney. On the other hand, he was later taken in by his wife's sham "automatic writing," profound texts allegedly produced in a hypnotic state and which became the basis for his philosophical treatise *The Vision*.

Yeats's gift, as W. H. Auden wrote (page 234), survived all this silliness. In fact his searching and voracious intellect, though at times indiscriminate, is essential to his gift. Age did not blunt his energy or make him complacent, and neither did the Nobel Prize he was awarded in 1923. In his later life, still a moderate nationalist, he served as a senator in the quasi-independent Irish Free State and then as a sort of freelance political consultant. He died in France, and his body was returned to Ireland after the Second World War.

The Silver Apples of the Moon, the Golden Apples of the Sun

Though I am old with wandering
Through hollow lands and hilly lands,
I will find out where she has gone,
And kiss her lips and take her hands;
And walk among long dappled grass,
And pluck till time and times are done
The silver apples of the moon,
The golden apples of the sun.

"The Song of Wandering Aengus" (1899),
17–24

From the beginning to the end of his career, Yeats built poems on the dreamy and mysterious ground of myth. This haunting poem, though infrequently anthologized, is a beautiful example of what Yeats could do with a simple but very strange fairy tale.

As the poem begins, a man named Aengus, prompted by some unknown notion, sets out for a hazel grove. He builds a little fishing rod out of a stick, a thread, and a berry, and at dawn he fishes a "little silver trout" from a stream.

But this is no ordinary trout. While his back is turned, it metamorphoses into a "glimmering girl / With apple blossom in her hair," who calls his name and then fades into "the brightening air." Such an episode would change anyone's life, and in Aengus's case it turns him into an eternal seeker—thus the epithet "Wandering Aengus."

For Aengus the girl represents a kind of eternal, supernatural peace. He envisions finding her one day, and when he does he believes he will escape time and space. They will walk in the dappled grass beyond the end of time, and somehow travel beyond the reaches of Earth, to pluck "The silver apples of the moon,/ The golden apples of the sun."

These final lines are among Yeats's most quotable, though the poem is not very famous. The penultimate line, in particular, has taken on a second life as the title of a pioneering work of electronic music by Morton Subotnick (1967).

A Terrible Beauty Is Born

I have met with them at close of day
Coming with vivid faces
From counter or desk among gray
Eighteenth-century houses.
I have passed with a nod of the head
Or polite meaningless words,
Or have lingered awhile and said
Polite meaningless words,
And thought before I had done
Of a mocking tale or a gibe
To please a companion
Around the fire at the club,
Being certain that they and I
But lived where motley is worn:
All changed, changed utterly:
A terrible beauty is born.

"Easter 1916" (1916), 1–16

Easter Sunday, 1916, is a day of infamy in annals of Irish nationalism. On that day a motley crew called Sinn Fein ("We Ourselves") led a national rebellion against British rule over the island—an event soon known as the Easter Rebellion.

The British response was powerful and swift, and after putting the uprising down they executed many of the rebel leaders. These included Patrick Pearse, Thomas MacDonagh, John MacBride, and James Connolly, all of whom Yeats knew and all of whom appear in this poem.

Before the rebellion and its terrible outcome, however, Yeats did not particularly admire these characters. In fact, he generally thought them fools, the sort of people to joke about at the club. ("Motley" is the fool's garb in a Shakespearean comedy.) They seemed, as Yeats puts it later, like characters in a "casual comedy."

But after the rebellion, "All changed, changed utterly." However flawed the raw matter of their characters, these players were transformed by action. They embodied, in rising up, a spirit both beautiful (like the ideal of freedom) and terrible (like the bloody reality). This "terrible beauty," born on Easter, survived their deaths—though I hesitate to guess what Yeats would have thought of the current situation in Northern Ireland.

Though he was fascinated by violent heroism, and hopelessly smitten with the radical nationalist Maud Gonne, Yeats wasn't exactly Sinn Fein material. In fact, as he grew older he inclined further to the Protestant side, often supporting their cause as a senator in the Irish Free State (later the Republic of Ireland) established by Britain in 1922.

WILLIAM BUTLER YEATS

Things Fall Apart; the Centre Cannot Hold

> Turning and turning in the widening gyre
> The falcon cannot hear the falconer;
> Things fall apart; the centre cannot hold;
> Mere anarchy is loosed upon the world,
> The blood-dimmed tide is loosed, and every-
>   where
> The ceremony of innocence is drowned;
> The best lack all conviction, while the worst
> Are full of passionate intensity.

> "The Second Coming" (1920), 1–8

Though this line has been quoted to death, in context it still has incredible power. Yeats means more than "arrangements disintegrate," though he is making a sort of universal statement—the literary equivalent of the law of entropy. More specifically, he's lamenting Europe's political state in 1920.

Everywhere he looked—including his native Ireland—Yeats saw dangerous demagogues rising to power. Russia had suffered the "blood-dimmed tide" of revolution three years earlier, with the Bolsheviks triumphant; and there were ominous political movements spawning, for example, in Italy and Germany.

Yeats related these events to a universal historical cycle, which he symbolized in the "gyre," a central image in his somewhat odd mystical philosophy. What the gyre actually looks like—a pair of cones, a figure eight, a spiral—seems to change with every text. In this case we may think of it as a spiral, symbolizing the tendency of history to repeat as it advances. Civilizations rise and fall, learning increases and is extinguished, chaos gives way to order, and then order to chaos.

In the first line of "The Second Coming," he figures the historical gyre as the flight of a falcon spiraling ever further from its "centre," the falconer, threatening to break free of his control. As he saw it, historical events were also spiraling free of the present order, the liberal political "centre" of Western civilization. Those who—like the Mensheviks—embodied that order were weak and uninspiring, while its opponents were filled with a dangerous, crowd-pleasing intensity.

Yeats's poem was eerily prophetic of the chaos that would come again in the '30s, but we shouldn't make too much of his premonitions. After all, Western culture survived; and while fascism and communism are hardly dead, they're not likely to loose any blood-dimmed tides too soon.

To Slouch towards Bethlehem

Surely some revelation is at hand;
Surely the Second Coming is at hand.
The Second Coming! Hardly are those words out
When a vast image out of Spiritus Mundi
Troubles my sight: somewhere in the sands of the
    desert
A shape with lion body and the head of a man,
A gaze blank and pitiless as the sun,
Is moving its slow thighs, while all about it
Reel shadows of the indignant desert birds.
The darkness drops again; but now I know
That twenty centuries of stony sleep

Were vexed to nightmare by a rocking cradle,
And what rough beast, its hour come round at
    last,
Slouches towards Bethlehem to be born?

    "The Second Coming" (1920), 9–22

As we saw in the previous entry, Yeats believed that history is governed by an eternal cycle, turning round and round in a "gyre." And if all things return, and the end of a cycle is at hand, then perhaps we are on the verge of a "Second Coming"—only this time not so nice.

In fact, as soon as Yeats entertains the idea, his mind is filled with horrible images, supplied by *Spiritus Mundi,* "the soul of the world," Yeats's equivalent of the collective unconscious. He sees a figure—a rough beast, half-lion, half-man—slowly moving through a desert, "Slouch[ing] towards Bethlehem to be born."

Obviously, Yeats is referring to the birth of Christ roughly "twenty centuries" ago. What he fears is that this turn of the historical gyre will bring the birth of a nightmarish antichrist and a reign of irrationality. Yeats didn't believe in a literal beast; an influential group of really bad people would do.

How Can We Know the Dancer from the Dance?

Labor is blossoming or dancing where
The body is not bruised to pleasure soul,
Nor beauty born out of its own despair,
Nor blear-eyed wisdom out of midnight oil.
O chestnut tree, great-rooted blossomer,
Are you the leaf, the blossom, or the bole?
O body swayed to music, O brightening glance,
How can we know the dancer from the dance?

"Among School Children" (1927), 57–64

In a mere 64 lines, Yeats breathlessly runs an almost ridiculous gamut of perplexities, including (among others): how two people can be spiritually one; how one can grasp another's past; how memories affect present perceptions; whether we have sensations before birth, and whether we retain them; what a mother would think if she could see her aged son; whether Plato, Aristotle, or Pythagoras had any real clue; what the source is of creativity; how art is or isn't like nature; how parts relate to wholes; how we identify what is essential; and, finally and most famously, "How can we know the dancer from the dance?"

Obviously, "Among School Children"—a record of the 60–year-old poet's myriad thoughts upon visiting a Catholic grade school—is rather compressed, and so it has its difficult moments. This last stanza, for instance, is difficult to understand down to the detail. But what Yeats says, more or less, is that truly fruitful, truly joyous, and truly natural creation requires inner harmony.

If the will, or "soul," presses the body into painful labor, the result cannot be natural and harmonious. Likewise if the soul is in pain, even though there might be beauty in despair's expression. Nor can sheer intellectual effort yield true art, for it cuts out the physical half of experience. Yeats's ideal of art is a completely unified, seamless expression, which, like the objects of nature's art, cannot be reduced to any single part.

Yeats beautifully sums up this train of thought in his last two verses. In the image of the dancer completely absorbed in her dance—soul and body joyfully at one with music—he finds a symbol for art indivisible, creator at one with creation, actor with action, producer with process. The dance isn't something external to the dancer: it is not an object we can isolate, an expression detached from motive. Nor is the dancer really that dancer except as realized and fulfilled in the dance.

All this goes back to what Yeats thinks he's doing in this poem. He isn't simply riffing on a set of interesting ideas; he's attempting to fully inhabit the language, to become one and harmonious with the act of writing, which expresses him as much as he expresses it. The sudden appearances and disappearances of notions, the complex weaving of associations, the shifting shades of feeling and thought, all embody and realize a living sensibility. He succeeded well enough; "Among School Children" is universally considered one of the greatest poetic dances in English.

The 20th Century

Between the turn of the century and the outbreak of war in 1939, English-language poetry took a number of turns, generally in the direction of the difficult. Traditional forms were discarded in a quest for new ones that would reflect the times, and these unfamiliar forms were often elusively symbolic.

It was a time when old certainties were shattered and old values put into question. Events such as the First World War, the Great Depression, and the rise of fascism, and theories such as those of Freud and Einstein, made the world seem increasingly hard to fathom, and certainty ever more uncertain. Artists and poets stepped into the breach, claiming lofty new roles for art and the imagination, exploring the subtleties and mysteries of human perspective, promising a world more real than reality. Poets such as T. S. Eliot and his legions of imitators wrote like prophets, with an accompanying gloom and obscurity. Meanwhile, fewer people were listening.

Modernist poetry like Eliot's, erudite and formally ambitious, is indeed difficult and at times almost hostile; but not all modern poetry is as hard to read as most people think. There's nothing obscure in Kipling (would that some of it were), or for that matter in Frost, who follows Wordsworth in writing in the common idiom.

And even a lot of the difficult stuff is difficult because readers approach it in fear, as if they are going to be quizzed on what it "means." (Teachers, more than poets, have killed off the taste for poetry.) Even if you can't explain a poem, you can still experience it. Poetry is basically imaginative play, a joy in the *feel* of ideas and sounds. Sometimes poems make statements, sometimes they capture the motions of feeling and thought, sometimes they just show off how prettily the poet can write. The meaning is as much in the performance of poetry as in its statements, which may clarify on repeated reading or which may never clarify. But this is not a failure.

Some of the poems discussed in this chapter were actually written before 1900, as their author's work spanned the turn of the century. The cut-off date is 1939, an equally arbitrary figure but one that allows for at least a little historical perspective. The roster of poets includes:

RUDYARD KIPLING (1865–1936): born in India, educated in England, a journalist back in India, and a propagandist back in England; writer of charming stories for young people and jingoistic poems for adults;

A. E. HOUSMAN (1859–1936): revived the grand English tradition of pastoral poetry; lamented inhumane secular and religious laws that condemned him, as a homosexual, to a life of frustration; lyric poet of simple country joy and of practically suicidal depression;

ROBERT FROST (1874–1963): born in San Francisco; lived in Massachusetts, New Hampshire, and London before teaching at Amherst; by most accounts an unpleasant man; an aesthetic conservative who ignored poetic trends; read a poem at John F. Kennedy's inaugural;

WALLACE STEVENS (1879–1955): an insurance executive by day and poet by night; author of perhaps the most difficult, but also perhaps the most exciting, modern American poetry;

MARIANNE MOORE (1887–1972): raised in St. Louis, educated at Bryn Mawr; author of sharp, funny, irregular poems on animals and everyday subjects; an influential literary editor in the '20s; fond of three-cornered hats;

WILLIAM CARLOS WILLIAMS (1883–1963): a New Jersey doctor who began writing poems after meeting H. D. and Ezra Pound at the University of Pennsylvania; wrote colloquial poetry about "man with nothing but the thing and the feeling of that thing"; an enormous influence on contemporary American poetry;

W. H. AUDEN (1907–1973): the first great English poet who was truly of the 20th century; a formal master whose work could be facile, but which was also intelligent, psychologically acute, witty, and moving; fled England for New York just before the beginning of World War II, and subsequently recanted much of his earlier (leftist) poetry, calling it "insincere."

The Female of the Species Is More Deadly Than the Male

> Man's timid heart is bursting with the things he
>   must not say,
> For the Woman that God gave him isn't his to
>   give away;
> But when the hunter meets with husband, each
>   confirms the other's tale—
> The female of the species is more deadly than the
>   male.
>
> Rudyard Kipling, "The Female of
> the Species" (1911), 13–16

Rudyard Kipling—beloved author of such popular stories as *Captains Courageous*, *Kim*, and *The Jungle Book*—also wrote nearly 700 poems. You'd hardly know it, though, since they're seldom reprinted. Although Kipling coined some eternal phrases—such as "the white man's burden" and "never the twain shall meet"—the poems are themselves often dreary, sometimes distasteful, and politically very incorrect.

A good example is "The Female of the Species," which you'd be hard pressed to find in any modern anthology. Its premise is that whether you're talking about bears, snakes, or human beings, you can expect no mercy from females. According to Kipling, males will avoid conflict; but females will promptly rip you to pieces. The only difference among species is that human females usually go for the psyche.

The reason, Kipling says with indeterminate irony, is that God built females for two purposes: to be "Mother of the Infant and the Mistress of the Mate." Especially when it comes to her children, the female is driven by a powerful and savage protective instinct that allows no room for hesitation or doubt. Whenever she senses danger, her instincts make her instantly lash out.

Males, on the other hand, have no such instinct, which leaves them prone to laziness, fear, compromise, and silly abstractions like "Justice." Kipling, again with a slippery sort of irony, condemns men for letting "Fear, or foolishness" deter them from promptly extinguishing the wicked. "Doubt and Pity oft perplex / Him in dealing with an issue—to the scandal of the Sex!" Timid Man cannot even speak his mind in the presence of his Woman, who when angered is capable of "Scientific vivisection of one nerve till it is raw."

Ironical or not, Kipling's theory is blatantly sexist, not to mention racist. (He treats American Indians as a species apart from Europeans.) In fact there are a lot of charges you could level at the poem, except that the poetry itself is so disarming. In other words, unlike the dreary "White Man's Burden," this poem is fun.

Be Still, My Soul

> Be still, my soul, be still; the arms you bear are
>   brittle,
>   Earth and high heaven are fixt of old and
>   founded strong.
> Think rather,—call to thought, if now you grieve
>   a little,
>   The days when we had rest, O soul, for they
>   were long.

A. E. Housman, *A Shropshire Lad* (1896),
lxviii, 1–4

A. E. Housman was a poet of emotion, frequently depressing and sometimes morbid. In this poem his speaker—a young man from Shropshire—wrestles with feelings of pain and rage, attempting to still the commotion in his heart.

What's got the lad's soul in a roil is some unspecified, unjust unkindness, and it hurts him bad. He tries to rise above the pain by thinking back to the days when he and his soul "had rest"—not in this lifetime, but "in days ere I was born." As the poem proceeds his self-pity grows, and he longs more for the comfort of that prenatal oblivion. "Oh why did I awake?" he cries; "when shall I sleep again?" End of poem.

"Be still, my soul" is a line now quoted with mock melodrama. It is a bit absurd to try reasoning with one's own soul, but then again English poetry is full of such absurdities. Housman gets picked on because his sincerity is unrelieved by any apparent irony. His earnest poetry can be simple and lovely, but sometimes it just seems silly.

A World He Never Made

> And how am I to face the odds
> Of man's bedevilment and God's?
> I, a stranger and afraid
> In a world I never made.

> Housman, *Last Poems* (1922), xii, 15–18

It's easy to understand why Housman, secretly homosexual and atheistic to boot, felt a little alienated. He'd have had a bad enough time today, let alone in his own culture. And while he steered clear of trouble (and of people in general), he fiercely resented what he calls in this poem "The laws of God, the laws of man."

Here's his argument against them: Mind your own business. He doesn't like a lot of the things so-called law-abiding, God-fearing men may do; but he isn't passing laws against *them*. "Please yourselves, say I, and they / Need only look the other way." But of course they won't; "they must still / Wrest their neighbor to their will."

After this, Housman's rebellion sort of fizzles out. What chance does he have against a whole society, he a stranger and afraid in a world he never made? Very little; so he sensibly gives up. Having another talk with his soul, he notes that "we cannot fly / To Saturn nor to Mercury" to make a world of their own. So they'll just have to keep, "if keep we can / These foreign laws of God and man." Sensible, but still kind of a letdown.

Home Is Where They Have to Take You In

"Warren," she said, "he has come home to die:
You needn't be afraid he'll leave you this time."

"Home," he mocked gently.

          "Yes, what else but home?
It all depends on what you mean by home.
Of course he's nothing to us, any more
Than was the hound that came a stranger to us

～⤫～

Out of the woods, worn out upon the trail."

"Home is the place where, when you have to go
     there,
They have to take you in."

          "I should have called it
Something you somehow haven't to deserve."

> Robert Frost, "The Death of the
> Hired Man" (1914), 111–20

A short story in verse, "The Death of the Hired Man" is an argument between Warren and his wife, Mary, over the fate of Silas, an old and not very useful hired hand. You will not be shocked to learn that Silas dies in the end.

By giving that away, Frost keeps the focus on the argument. Silas has shown up exhausted and disoriented at Warren and Mary's farm, where he's worked many times in the past, though with increasingly meager results. His pay was equally meager—just room and board—so at the busiest times he left to find a better deal. Warren has vowed never to take him back, but when he arrives broken at the door, Mary can't bear to turn him away.

As the poem begins, Warren and Mary are at odds: He thinks of Silas as a worthless and disloyal laborer; she thinks of him as a member of the family. But as the poem proceeds, Mary softens Warren up, and in the passage quoted here he's beginning to lose his conviction. "Home," he jokes cynically, "is the place where, when you have to go there, / They have to take you in." Warren sees home as an obligation, and he claims to feel no obligation to Silas. Mary counters that home is rather about heart: It's not something you have to earn.

Deep down Warren understands Mary's point, so he eventually comes around, though only in time to discover Silas's lifeless body. And his famous line is never quoted seriously. Parents just like to pretend sometimes that they're only doing their children a favor.

The Road Less Traveled

I shall be telling this with a sigh
Somewhere ages and ages hence:
Two roads diverged in a wood, and I—
I took the one less traveled by,
And that has made all the difference.

Frost, "The Road Not Taken" (1916), 16–20

❧

In recent years we've heard lots about roads less traveled, those inconvenient routes to virtue. We almost never hear of roads less traveled *by,* which is what the phrase's author said.

Maybe Frost wanted to be precise (not traveled *over,* not traveled *down,* but traveled *by*); maybe he fell victim to his rhyme scheme. Either way, *traveled by* is what he wrote. The original may sound wrong to our ears today; but well before anyone heard of M. Scott Peck, this was one of America's best-loved poems.

Peck was right about one thing: Frost is talking about more than just a road. This is a poem about decisions and how we come to doubt them later. The speaker arrives at a fork in the road and wishes he didn't have to choose which way to turn, since both roads look so nice. After some comparison and hesitation he chooses the one less worn by traffic.

As the speaker admits, the real difference between the roads is very slight—"the passing there / Had worn them really about the same." Yet somehow the choice becomes a major event in his life, the stuff of some personal legend. As he stands there debating which way to turn, he thinks of how "way leads on to way," each fork leading to later branches, small diversions cascading into different futures. You can imagine how this might work: "If I hadn't taken the left road, I wouldn't have stopped at that inn; and if I hadn't stopped at that inn, I wouldn't have met my future wife," and so on.

Frost's speaker doesn't tell any story like this; he never tells us why taking the road less traveled by made so great a difference. It doesn't matter; this isn't a poem about what happened next. It's a poem about the moment of choice, the wish to travel both roads at once, and the melancholy fact that every possible future excludes at least one other. The speaker apparently wishes now he had taken the road more traveled by, but of course nobody can know where that would have left him— probably wishing he'd taken the other.

Some Say the World Will End in Fire, Some Say in Ice

> Some say the world will end in fire,
> Some say in ice.
> From what I've tasted of desire
> I hold with those who favor fire.
> But if I had to perish twice,
> I think I know enough of hate
> To say that for destruction ice
> Is also great
> And would suffice.

Frost, "Fire and Ice" (1923)

Some like it hot, and that goes for the apocalypse too. I don't know who Frost's authorities were, but he presumes for the sake of the poem that Earth's extinction will be either fiery or icy. And I don't know who told him he'd be around for the event, but he first elects fire, and for the second time ice.

Here's where things get a little complicated. Obviously, neither a person nor a world can perish twice, let alone perish simultaneously. Frost is really just conducting a thought experiment, which turns out to be more about human passion than personal or global death. (And global death is a lot more fun to contemplate.)

The poet, having personally never been burned to death, imagines the possibility in terms of something he knows: the fiery feeling of all-consuming desire. At first the idea is attractive: Passion has a lot going for it, especially compared to its opposite—icy indifference or disdain.

This would seem to complete the ratio—desire is to fire as hate is to ice. But why, if the speaker survives the flames of passion, would he choose icy hatred the second time around? The answer is left to the reader as an excercise.

You may, however, read the poem a completely different way. There's a thin line between love and hate, which may burn as well as freeze—and it's a more potent destroyer when it burns. If this is how Frost is thinking, then what he's really saying is that while fire seems attractive at first (as desire), it loses its appeal when it slips into hatred and smolders. In which case, icy indifference is looking good.

Miles to Go before I Sleep

> The woods are lovely, dark and deep,
> But I have promises to keep,
> And miles to go before I sleep,
> And miles to go before I sleep.
>
> Frost, "Stopping by Woods on a Snowy
> Evening" (1923), 13–16

This small, unaffected poem has become famous and often quoted for what many see as its profound symbolism.

What Frost calls "sleep," for example, is widely interpreted as death. This popular take on its meaning, however, is purely in the beholder's eye; and even if it weren't, there are lots of profoundly symbolic poems nobody reads, let alone quotes. What sells Frost's poem is that it's so easy while seeming so deep. Sometimes deceptive simplicity is really just plain old simplicity.

Just because a poem means what it says doesn't make it bad. Frost, quite capable both of profundity and symbolism, is one of the great American poets mostly because of his straightforward, vernacular style. Often he wrote just to capture ordinary experience, and that's the case with "Stopping by Woods on a Snowy Evening."

Symbolism aside, what we have here is a traveler quite literally stopping by woods on a snowy evening. He pulls up in his horse for a moment of quiet and peace, which he finds in the lovely view of snow falling on the dark, deep woods. But he cannot linger, since he still has business to attend to and miles to travel before he can get to bed.

And that's more or less it; there is no direct clue in the poem of a secondary meaning. True, there's something disturbing and mysterious about the last stanza, which I quote here. But it's ordinary weariness and an ordinary sense of loss to which Frost lends those qualities. The greatness of this poem is to suggest the depth of feeling we find even in ordinary moments.

Thirteen Ways of Looking at a Blackbird

I
Among twenty snowy mountains,
The only moving thing
Was the eye of a blackbird.

II
I was of three minds,
Like a tree
In which there are three blackbirds.

III
The blackbird whirled in the autumn winds.
It was a small part of the pantomime.

IV
A man and a woman
Are one.
A man and a woman and a blackbird
Are one.

Wallace Stevens, "Thirteen Ways of Looking
at a Blackbird" (1917), 1–12

Some say Wallace Stevens was *the* great American poet of the 20th century. I'm inclined to agree; but on the other hand Stevens has never been popular—your average reader would find it difficult to quote even one of his lines. The closest he comes to fame is this poem, particularly its title, which has often been imitated or parodied. (A recent headline from the *San Francisco Chronicle*: "W. H. Auden: Ten Ways of Looking at a Poet.")

༁

Stevens, a Connecticut insurance executive by day, wrote difficult, allusive poetry by night. His work is more or less *sui generis,* though like every poet he had his influences, and like every poet responded to the intellectual and aesthetic fashions of his day. "Thirteen Ways" (four quoted here) takes off on the contemporary taste for haiku, which also inspired poems by Ezra Pound and William Carlos Williams.

The poem—or, as Stevens called it, "this group of poems"—also responds to contemporary experiments in multiple perspective, such as Cubist painting. You might think a blackbird is just a blackbird; and, at the level of raw existence, you're right. But we don't perceive raw existence; it gets filtered through our senses and meddled with by our brains. Perception is never pure; we see things from an angle, or even from a variety of angles; sensations take on meaning only as they find a place in our imaginations.

Stevens gives us thirteen possible views of a blackbird, though he could probably have given us a hundred. In each the bird "means" something different depending on where it fits in the mental landscape. In the first view, for example, the tiny eye of a blackbird gains an enormous intensity when set against the vast stillness of twenty snowy mountains. In the second and fourth views, the bird is a metaphor or symbol for abstract entities such as thought and being.

The poem is certainly philosophical, but it would be a mistake to overanalyze it. Stevens later wrote that it is not "a collection of epigrams or ideas, but of sensations." In other words, you're allowed to just feel it.

❧

Imaginary Gardens with Real Toads in Them

> One must make a distinction
> however: when dragged into prominence by
> half poets, the result is not poetry,
> nor till the poets among us can be
> 'literalists of
> the imagination'—above
> insolence and triviality and can present
> for inspection, 'imaginary gardens with real toads
> in them,' shall we have
> it.

Marianne Moore, "Poetry" (1921), 18–25

One of the great modern essays on verse is Marianne Moore's self-reflexive poem "Poetry," also one of her better-known (if hardly famous) works. "I, too, dislike it," she disarmingly begins, as if replying to a common explanation for why most people don't read poetry. She considers most of it "fiddle," and sensibly notes that "we / do not admire what / we cannot understand."

Moore demands something more than the "insolence and triviality" of so much poetry, which is unintelligible noise about nothing very important. She demands the "genuine," the real stuff of life, things that matter to everyone and not just to poets. The genuine includes everything from "a wild horse taking a roll" to baseball and business documents: "all these phenomena are important."

On the other hand, it doesn't suffice simply to drag these subjects into poems, for true poetry still demands literary skill and imaginative precision. True poetry is made

up of "imaginary gardens with real toads in them"—
vividly realized fictions with genuine content, the real elevated through what she called "heightened consciousness."

Moore didn't just preach about imaginary gardens
with real toads; she practiced. She made poetry from common objects and experiences, as in such works as "To a
Steam Roller," "Four Quartz Crystal Clocks," "Granite
and Steel," "Old Amusement Park," "Blue Bug," "Carnegie
Hall: Rescued," and "Sun." Along with W. H. Auden and
W. C. Williams, Moore helped bring the stuff of everyday
modern life into poetry, and to make it poetic.

So Much Depends upon a Red Wheel Barrow

so much depends
upon

a red wheel
barrow

glazed with rain
water

beside the white
chickens

William Carlos Williams, "The Red
Wheelbarrow" (1923)

While T. S. Eliot made his way to England, and Ezra
Pound to Italy, William Carlos Williams was the poet who
stayed in America. Like Eliot, Williams was a friend of

Pound's; and like both he believed new times required a new poetry: sharp, precise, unromantic. But unlike Pound and Eliot, Williams, a practicing doctor in Rutherford, New Jersey, didn't turn to the past for his themes and models. He drew his matter from ordinary life, and he wrote in colloquial American English.

"No ideas but in things," Williams famously said in *Paterson*, his sprawling epic about a nearby city. Poetry shouldn't philosophize, it should present: It should show, not tell. This poem about a red wheelbarrow is the best-known specimen of Williams's technique. Only the first line comes anywhere near an idea; the rest is just basic reporting.

There's nothing terribly remarkable about your average red wheelbarrow. The first line—"so much depends"—is sort of a setup; if the third line surprises you, that's what Williams intended. What's remarkable about the poem, with its unexpected twists and strange word arrangement, is that Williams makes an ordinary wheelbarrow remarkable—the stuff of poetry. Each new line, while following from the last, gives a little jolt, lending a strange intensity to the poet's perceptions.

And, in truth, much *does* depend on ordinary objects and ordinary events—they're just not the usual subjects of poetry. Neither are cities in New Jersey the stuff of epics, which just goes to prove Williams's dedication to the marvels of the ordinary.

꩜

Poetry Makes Nothing Happen

You were silly like us; your gift survived it all:
The parish of rich women, physical decay,
Yourself. Mad Ireland hurt you into poetry.
Now Ireland has her madness and her weather
    still,
For poetry makes nothing happen: it survives
In the valley of its making where executives
Would never want to tamper, flows on south
From ranches of isolation and the busy griefs,
Raw towns that we believe and die in; it survives,
A way of happening, a mouth.

W. H. Auden, "In Memory of
W. B. Yeats" (1939), 31–40

Wystan Hugh Auden was apparently quite a character—eccentric, foul-mouthed, compulsive, slovenly, brilliant, and perverse. He loved obscure old words (the *OED* was his favorite book) and equally loved the latest slang. Some critics and readers think he's the greatest, others find him a bore. It's too soon to know what history will say; but it's certain that no one will memorialize him the way he memorialized Yeats.

The poem is full of brilliant, chilling lines ("What instruments we have agree / The day of his death was a dark cold day") and quotable aphorisms ("he became his admirers"). Probably the most commonly quoted, though, is "poetry makes nothing happen." This is a sad truth for a poet to admit, but a pertinent one for poets in wartime—Yeats at the Easter Rebellion (page 209), Auden on the eve of the Second World War.

But this isn't to say that poetry is useless. It may not alter the course of history, but it can alter how we tell it. Yeats could do nothing in verse to quell the strife of "Mad Ireland," but he gave lasting voice ("a mouth") to certain sufferings and sentiments. It's true that Yeats bought into silly mystical theories, and that he was rather cozy with the society of wealth, but those things are gone and his gift remains, the poetry that may *make* nothing happen, but that defines the *way* it happened.

T. S. Eliot

Born in St. Louis in 1888, Thomas Stearns Eliot spent his adult life in England, thus giving two countries cause to claim him as their own. Whether he was the greatest poet of this century is arguable; but his masterpiece, *The Waste Land* (1921), is without doubt the classic Modernist poem. Its difficulty, its depth, its irony, its epochal resonance, and its fame put it in a class otherwise inhabited only by Joyce's equally definitive novel, *Ulysses,* published the same year.

Eliot left the States while working on his Harvard dissertation in Hegelian philosophy. After a short period of study in Paris, he attended Oxford for a year and then became a schoolteacher in London. Just before assuming his teaching duties in 1915, he published his first great work, "The Love Song of J. Alfred Prufrock," a symbol-laden portrait of the alienated modern man. In addition to poems he also wrote book reviews and literary essays, setting forth some of the basic tenets of what would be called "the New Criticism," a formalist movement which dominated American criticism in the 1940s and '50s.

In *The Waste Land* Eliot captured Europe's cultural fragmentation and spiritual exhaustion in the aftermath of World War I. It also reflected personal feelings of rootlessness and spiritual hollowness, feelings that eventually led him to embrace the traditions and official religion of his adopted country. In 1927 he simultaneously became a British subject and a devout Anglican, and his best works of the 1930s and '40s—such as "Ash Wednesday" (1930) and *Four Quartets* (1935–43)—are meditations on faith and celebrations of order.

Though *The Waste Land* is Eliot's masterpiece, its disjointedness and frequent obscurity (which caused him to add footnotes for book publication) make it a poem more studied than read. Readers still enjoy "Prufrock" and admire the *Quartets,* but by far his most popular work today is *Old Possum's Book of Practical Cats,* a collection of children's poetry published in 1939. Eliot also wrote five philosophical-religious plays, including *Murder in the Cathedral* (1935), which were popular in the 1950s and which are still occasionally performed today. He died in 1965.

Let Us Go Then, You and I...

Let us go then, you and I,
When the evening is spread out against the sky
Like a patient etherized upon a table;
Let us go, through certain half-deserted streets,
The muttering retreats
Of restless nights in one-night cheap hotels
And sawdust restaurants with oyster shells:
Streets that follow like a tedious argument
Of insidious intent
To lead you to an overwhelming question...
Oh, do not ask, "What is it?"
Let us go and make our visit.

In the room the women come and go
Talking of Michelangelo.

"The Love Song of J. Alfred Prufrock"
(1915), 1–14

These opening lines of T. S. Eliot's first great poem set the scene in a seedy and depressing modern city—or rather, in a city that seems seedy and depressing to the speaker, J. Alfred Prufrock, an overeducated nobody and a middle-aged social failure. The city is nameless, as is the "you" he addresses; most likely there's no "you" at all, and what we're hearing is a sad internal monologue.

The first three lines, often quoted just to prove that the quoter has read the poem, capture Prufrock's weary numbness, which for Eliot epitomizes a brand of modern alienation. In the "etherized" (anaesthetized) evening, Prufrock wonders whether it's worth braving the depressing city streets—with their cheap hotels, bad restaurants, and air of anxiety—to pay meaningless social visits.

Actually, the question introduced in line 10 is more than whether it's worth leaving home, which isn't all that "overwhelming." But we never get the answer to "What is it?"—Prufrock tries to cut short a train of thought that seems to be heading in an even more depressing direction. Let's just go, he says to "you," or to himself; forget about why, and forget about whether there's really a point to anything.

However, it's unclear whether he ever really *does* get out the door. Though suddenly we seem to be at a party where women walk about discussing Renaissance sculpture, it may all be in his mind. And indeed a few stanzas later he's still debating what to do, trapped in self-conscious agonizing over his appearance (his bald spot, his deficient physique), wondering whether he'll have anything to say. Prufrock's "love song"—an ironic name—is really a song about his paralysis.

I Grow Old…I Grow Old…

No! I am not Prince Hamlet, nor was meant to
    be;
Am an attending lord, one that will do
To swell a progress, start a scene or two,
Advise the prince; no doubt, an easy tool,
Deferential, glad to be of use,
Politic, cautious, and meticulous;
Full of high sentence, but a bit obtuse;
At times, indeed, almost ridiculous—
Almost, at times, the Fool.

I grow old…I grow old…
I shall wear the bottoms of my trousers rolled.

Shall I part my hair behind? Do I dare to eat a
   peach?
I shall wear white flannel trousers, and walk upon
   the beach.
I have heard the mermaids singing, each to each.

I do not think they will sing to me.

> "The Love Song of J. Alfred Prufrock,"
> 111–25

A common technique in Eliot's early poems is sudden contrast, in which, for example, the grand and sublime are set side by side with the trivial and mundane. Prufrock's psyche is virtually defined by this technique; his thoughts jump from the universe to a coffee spoon, from Shakespeare to his trousers. All these things occupy his mind equally, while at the same time they're almost grotesquely discordant, emphasizing the gap between his dreams and his reality.

In reality, nobody dreams of comparing him to Hamlet; the thought occurs only to him. He shares with the prince only his inability to act: Just as Hamlet agonized over killing Claudius, Prufrock agonizes over what to say at tea. Otherwise, Prufrock knows he's not meant for the part. He's less like a prince than like a flattering, insignificant courtier; an "easy tool" of the prince's whims; not very clever but still full of "sentence" (received wisdom); at times practically a Shakespearean fool. That is, he's more like Polonius.

From this literary height Prufrock descends again to agonizing over his age and his appearance. "I grow old…I grow old…" he muses in a mood of self-pity, imagining himself as an ever lonely, ever self-consciousness, ever indecisive figure. Should he affectedly roll up the bottoms of his trousers? How should he part his hair? Can he summon the courage to eat a peach? Is there nothing he can do without worrying first?

If Prufrock weren't so sensitive and latently romantic, there would be none of this bother—he could just live his meaningless little life. But he once hoped to be great, and he still has dreams of a life stranger and more passionate than the one he lives. The mermaids he imagines hearing on the beach are the sirens calling to this other life; he hears them, but he knows they are not calling him. He is condemned to know and to covet what he cannot have.

April Is the Cruellest Month

> April is the cruellest month, breeding
> Lilacs out of the dead land, mixing
> Memory and desire, stirring
> Dull roots with spring rain.

The Waste Land (1922), 1–4

The first line of this poem is Eliot's biggest hit number, recycled each year by dozens, if not hundreds, of desperate writers looking for a lead. Certainly April, like most other months, brings its share of annoyances, but it hardly lives up to Eliot's "cruellest."

The poet indulges in hyperbole, or at least willful negativity. April, as any sensible person knows, is certainly no worse than several other months I could name. But the poem's narrator thinks so, because he believes that oblivion is bliss.

The problem with April, to his mind, is that it's neither winter nor spring—neither truly wasted and dead, nor truly full and alive. Nature is beginning to revive, but its "dull roots" only gradually push forth new life through the "stony rubbish" (line 20) of "the dead land." These tentative and tantalizing signs of life provoke a similar gradual awakening of the spirit, a thirst for freshness and warmth, but without their satisfaction. It's thus a time of unfulfilled desires, aching sensations we were more comfortable forgetting we'd had.

As Eliot later admitted, *The Waste Land* is one big "piece of rhythmical grumbling." Its opening verses are a pessimist's parody of the beginning of another great poem with an entirely different attitude toward the "shoures soote" of April, *The Canterbury Tales* (page 15). Chaucer's narrator is quite glad to be rid of winter and cheerily leaves it behind. Eliot's narrator can't forget it, nor forget the slide into oblivion.

I Will Show You Fear in a Handful of Dust

What are the roots that clutch, what branches
    grow
Out of this stony rubbish? Son of man,
You cannot say, or guess, for you know only
A heap of broken images, where the sun beats,
And the dead tree gives no shelter, the cricket no
    relief,

And the dry stone no sound of water. Only
There is shadow under this red rock,
(Come in under the shadow of this red rock),
And I will show you something different from
    either
Your shadow at morning striding behind you
Or your shadow at evening rising to meet you;
I will show you fear in a handful of dust.

The Waste Land, 19–30

The Waste Land is full of narrators, disembodied voices
that deliver an anecdote or song, a sound bite from some
old book or a fragment of conversation. Most of the time
we have no idea who's saying what, or whether any two
narrators are the same. But this is the point; Eliot is
attempting to make the fragments of his culture, myths
and voices from past and present, blend and flow. Like
other writers and artists of his youth, Eliot was a joiner of
the disjointed, paradoxically unifying in one frame a set of
disunited perspectives.

And though on the surface the pieces of *The Waste
Land* are disconnected, they all converge on a central
experience and theme: that we're living in a desolate
spiritual wasteland. Eliot finds symbols for this experience in characters and props from a variety of myths and
legends. Tiresias, prophet of doom from the blighted
Thebes of *Oedipus Rex,* plays a major part; and in this
passage Eliot draws on the voice of another prophet, the
Hebrew Bible's Ezekiel, whom God salutes in the desert
as "Son of man."

Whether the speaker here is Tiresias or Ezekiel or
some other bad-news bearer isn't clear, and isn't really
important. Eliot's credo was that the poet should render

subjective feeling as impersonally and objectively as possible. The disembodied voice addresses everyman: Ask not who's tolling the bell, he's tolling it for thee.

And the prophet is definitely a downer. "Son of man," he says, including at least the male half of humanity, you don't know what anything means; you can't even answer basic questions. Stuck in a fragmented world, you have no coherent basis for knowledge. All you know is that you are spiritually vacant, that your world is dry and dead, and that this is a wasteland.

In case, upon spying the shadow under a rock, you thought you'd found relief from the punishing heat of your desert world, forget it. The prophet will follow you there to tell you something worse. He'll show you a handful of dust.

And what's so frightful about a handful of dust? It's *dead*; in fact, it's death in concrete form. "Ashes to ashes," notes the old *Book of Common Prayer;* "dust to dust." And beyond physical death it symbolizes spiritual death, the ebbing of feeling into numbness, the hollow centerpiece of Eliot's early poetry. "Whatever you feel now," the prophet says in effect, "will ultimately be extinguished."

It was not the happiest time in Eliot's life. He composed *The Waste Land* late in 1921 at a Swiss sanatorium, recuperating from a physical and mental collapse. Six years later he would embrace the Anglican church.

T. S. ELIOT

࿐

Not with a Bang but a Whimper

This is the way the world ends
This is the way the world ends
This is the way the world ends
Not with a bang but a whimper.

"The Hollow Men" (1925), 96–99

"The Hollow Men" is a title Eliot might have given to several of his early poems. Prufrock is a type of hollow man, and *The Waste Land* is full of them—the walking dead, "stuffed men" each with a "Headpiece filled with straw."

If you've been following our entries on Eliot's poetry, you probably know the score by now: As he looked at the modern world around him, he saw sterility, hollowness, and decay, which he chalked up in part to a loss of spiritual wholeness, a division of reason from feeling. In a famous 1921 essay on the 17th-century Metaphysical poets, he called this the "dissociation of sensibility," leading not only to bad poetry (beginning with Milton), but also to bad culture.

Toward the end of his doom-and-gloom phase, he summed up this thesis in "The Hollow Men," particularly in its last section. "Between the idea / And the reality," he writes, "Between the motion / And the act / Falls the Shadow." In the modern age feeling is divided from action; there is a dark, substanceless barrier or "Shadow" of death between "emotion" and "response." Nothing we do has force; nothing we do has meaning.

He concludes the poem with a chilling little nursery rhyme, set to the tune of "Here we go round the mulberry bush" (which Eliot quotes, though his plant is a prickly pear). Our world is heading toward death, though not by any sort of grand gesture or "bang"; we're no longer capable of that. Rather, our culture is merely going numb, fading out with a whimper.

Reading "The Hollow Men" makes you wonder what Eliot would have preferred. One sometimes gets the sense that he was hoping for a "bang" to jolt the world, which may partly explain his flirtation with fascism. (He never actually supported the fascist cause, unlike his friend Ezra Pound.) Eliot lived through the most volatile phase of the Cold War, and saw the development of weapons that were capable of literally ending the world with a bang. So far as I know, he wrote nothing on the subject.

Human Kind Cannot Bear Very Much Reality

> Go, said the bird, for the leaves were full of chil-
> dren,
> Hidden excitedly, containing laughter.
> Go, go, go, said the bird: human kind
> Cannot bear very much reality.
> Time past and time future
> What might have been and what has been
> Point to one end, which is always present.

> *Four Quartets:* "Burnt Norton" (1935), 40–43

Eliot's *Four Quartets* certainly sound more like good old poetry than the grim earlier work we've been looking at so far. Like the other three, the first of the quartets, "Burnt Norton," is much more fluid and lyrical, more traditional in every way; you can almost get away with skipping the footnotes.

"Time present and time past," begins the poem, "Are both perhaps present in time future, / And time future contained in time past." Time is the Big Subject throughout the work, in which Eliot explores the relation of normal diurnal experiences to spiritual experiences, which have a timeless quality. Eliot wonders whether time as we know it is just an illusion, and whether "all time is eternally present," and thus the course of history forever fixed, contained by and pointing to "one end." Yes, you guessed it: This "one end" is Eternal Spirit, or God.

Eliot doesn't simply declare the problem solved—after all, this is *Four Quartets,* not *One Solo.* He blends the philosophy with observations of events in time, such as the flight of a thrush through vibrant autumn air, and the games of children in fallen leaves. The thrush's call sounds like *go,* and then *go, go, go,* but whom is it commanding, and why? Does it speak to the children, or to the adults who watch them in their rose garden?

Eliot's answer is rather enigmatic. "Human kind," the bird explains, "Cannot bear very much reality." A great line, but given that the poem has so far dealt only with mystical queries and a pretty harmless piece of reality, it comes right out of the blue. (Actually, it might have come straight from *Murder in the Cathedral,* in which the phrase also appears and which Eliot wrote that same year.) Perhaps the bird is urging the children to keep playing while they can, because life won't always be so easy. Or perhaps it's advising Eliot to escape reality by going back to his poetry and his mystical queries.

References

Bartlett's Familiar Quotations, 16th edition, gen. ed. Justin Kaplan (Boston: Little, Brown, 1992).

A Chaucer Glossary, ed. Norman Davis et al. (Oxford: Oxford University Press, 1979).

Lewis Carroll, *The Annotated Alice*, ed. with notes by Martin Gardner (New York: World Publishing, 1960).

The Home Book of Quotations, Classical and Modern, 9th edition, ed. Burton Stevenson (New York: Dodd, Mead, 1964).

The New Princeton Encyclopedia of Poetry and Poetics, ed. Alex Preminger and T. V. F. Brogan (Princeton: Princeton University Press, 1993).

The Norton Anthology of English Literature, 5th edition, gen. ed. M. H. Abrams, 2 vols. (New York: W. W. Norton, 1986).

The Norton Anthology of Modern Poetry, 2nd edition, eds. Richard Ellmann and Robert O'Clair (New York: W. W. Norton, 1988).

The Oxford Companion to English Literature, 4th edition, eds. Sir Paul Harvey and Dorothy Eagle (Oxford: Oxford University Press, 1967).

The Oxford English Dictionary, 2nd edition (Oxford: Oxford University Press, 1989).

Shakespeare's Sonnets, ed. with commentary by Stephen Booth (New Haven: Yale University Press, 1977).

Richard Shenkman, *Legends, Lies, and Cherished Myths of American History* (New York: William Morrow, 1988).

Index

INDEX

Index

INDEX

RD4CC